I AM A CAMERA

I

GREENWOOD PRESS, PUBLISHERS
WESTPORT, CONNECTICUT

7

Am a Camera

A PLAY IN THREE ACTS

BY JOHN VAN DRUTEN

Adapted from the Berlin Stories of CHRISTOPHER ISHERWOOD

The Library of Congress cataloged this book as follows:

Van Druten, John, 1901–1957.
    I am a camera; a play in three acts. Adapted from The
Berlin stories of Christopher Isherwood. Westport, Conn.,
Greenwood Press [1971, °1952]

    182 p. illus. 23 cm.

     I. Isherwood, Christopher, 1904–   The Berlin stories. II. Title.

PR6043.A4 I 13   1971   822'.9'12   71–152613
ISBN 0-8371-6048-0   MARC

Library of Congress   71 [4]

Originally published in 1952 by Random House, Inc., New York

Reprinted with the permission of Random House, Inc.

Reprinted from an original copy in the collections of the
University of Southern Illinois Library

Reprinted in 1971 by Greenwood Press
a division of Congressional Information Service
88 Post Road West, Westport, Connecticut 06881

Library of Congress Catalog Card Number 71-152613

ISBN 0-8371-6048-0
Printed in the United States of America

10 9 8 7 6 5 4 3 2

To
DODIE
who started the whole thing

I AM A CAMERA *was first presented by Gertrude Macy, in association with Walter Starcke, at the Empire Theatre, New York City, on Wednesday, November 28, 1951, with the following cast:*

CHRISTOPHER ISHERWOOD	William Prince
FRÄULEIN SCHNEIDER	Olga Fabian
FRITZ WENDEL	Martin Brooks
SALLY BOWLES	Julie Harris
NATALIA LANDAUER	Marian Winters
CLIVE MORTIMER	Edward Andrews
MRS. WATSON-COURTNEIDGE	Catherine Willard

Staged by John van Druten

Setting by Boris Aronson

Costumes by Ellen Goldsborough

The play is in three acts and seven scenes.

The set, throughout, is a room in Fräulein Schneider's flat in Berlin in 1930, before the rise of the Hitler regime.

The action covers about four months.

ACT ONE

ACT ONE

Scene I

Scene: *The scene throughout is a room in* FRÄULEIN SCHNEIDER's *flat in Berlin around 1930.*

The bed is hidden, or partially so, behind curtains upstage. The door to the hall is in the right wall. Windows in the left wall.

The room is excessively German and middle-class. There is a tall, tiled stove with an angel on it. A washstand by the curtains, like a Gothic shrine. A best chair like a bishop's throne. Antlers make a kind of hatstand by the door. There is a small table for tea. A backless sofa, and an ottoman. A large table by the window piled with books, papers and notebooks. There are one or two good Medici prints on the walls, between heavy German engravings.

Time: *A summer afternoon. When the curtain rises, the stage is dark except for a light on* CHRISTOPHER ISHERWOOD, *seated alone at the table. He is in his twenties, English and untidy. He wears flannel trousers, very dirty, and a shirt. (He wears this throughout the play. The only change will be in his tie.) He is writing and smoking. Then he stops and reads over what he has written.*

CHRIS
(Reading aloud)
"In the last few days, there has been a lot of Nazi rioting in the streets, here in Berlin. They are getting bolder, more arrogant." *(He stops)* No, that's all wrong.

(He crumples the page and throws it aside)

3

That's not the right way to start. It's sheer journalism. I must explain who it is who is telling all this—a typical beach-comber of the big city. He comes to Berlin for the week end, stays on, runs out of money, starts giving English lessons. Now he sits in a rented room, waiting for something to happen—something that will help him understand what his life is all about.

(*Rises, pouring beer into a glass*)

When Lord Tennyson wanted to write a poem, they say he used to put himself into a mystic trance by just repeating his own name. Alfred Tennyson. Christopher Isherwood. Christopher Isherwood. Christopher Isherwood. I like the sound of my name. "Alone among the writers of his generation, Christopher Isherwood can be said to have achieved true greatness." Shut up, idiot. The only book I ever published got five reviews, all bad, and sold two hundred and thirty-three copies to date. And I haven't even started this new one, though I've been here six months already. (*Sits at the table again*) Well, you're going to start now, this minute. You're not leaving this chair until you do. Write "Chapter One."

(*Does so*)

Good. Now begin. Create something. Anything.

(*He writes, then reads*)

"I am a camera, with it's shutter open, quite passive. Some day all of this will have to.be developed, printed, fixed."

(*The lights come up on the room. There is a knock on the door*)

Who's that?

FRÄULEIN SCHNEIDER
(*Off*)

It is I, Herr Issyvoo.

CHRIS

Come in, Fräulein.

(*She comes in. She is a large, bosomy, German woman. She carries a lace tea-cloth.*)

FRÄULEIN SCHNEIDER

I bring you this tea-cloth. When you are having a lady guest, you can trust Schneiderschen to make things elegant. Now, where do you want all of these things to go, Herr Issyvoo?

CHRIS

Oh, put them on the floor.

FRÄULEIN SCHNEIDER

But you cannot put things on the floor.

CHRIS

There are a lot of things there already.

FRÄULEIN SCHNEIDER

But they must not stay there, not if a lady is coming. It does not look good at all.

CHRIS

You'd better put them on the bed. She won't be looking at the bed.

FRÄULEIN SCHNEIDER

And how do you know that, Herr Issyvoo? A handsome young man like you?

CHRIS

Fräulein Schneider, I'm surprised at you.

FRÄULEIN SCHNEIDER

(*With a big laugh*)

Oh, Herr Issyvoo, I have been young, too. Young and saucy.

(*Rather archly, she takes the things to the bed behind the curtains.*)

CHRIS

I suppose you had a great many admirers, Fräulein Schneider?

FRÄULEIN SCHNEIDER

Oh, I had dozens, Herr Issyvoo. But only one Friend. (*She returns for more stuff*) Eleven years we were together. Then he died. And it was after that that I became fat. The bosom, you know. It grew and it grew. I think it is still growing. And it is such a weight to carry about with you. It is like carrying a suitcase. *Two* suitcases. And it is sad that it should all have grown after he died. He was a man for bosoms. It would have made him so happy. And now it does no one any good. This young lady you are expecting—she is very attractive?

CHRIS

She is one of my pupils. She wanted to see where I lived. Though when I say she is one of my pupils, it isn't true. She's the only one I have left. The others have all gone away for the summer. Fräulein Schneider, I have got to have a talk with you.

FRÄULEIN SCHNEIDER

Ja, Herr Issyvoo?

CHRIS

I don't think I can go on living here.

FRÄULEIN SCHNEIDER

What? Oh, Herr Issyvoo, you are not going to leave me? Are you not comfortable here?

CHRIS

Yes, I am very comfortable. It's just that I can't afford it.

FRÄULEIN SCHNEIDER

Oh, that can wait.

CHRIS

No. It's been waiting too long. I haven't paid you for two months—not properly. I've got it here.
(*Takes money from wallet*)
I was just wondering—that little room across the passage —just across the passage—that's not let.

FRÄULEIN SCHNEIDER

But it is so small, Herr Issyvoo. Why, I can hardly get into it myself. And what do I do with this room? With the summer coming on, I shall never find a tenant for it.

CHRIS

Oh, I'm sure you will. And until you do, why don't you live in it yourself, instead of the sitting room?

FRÄULEIN SCHNEIDER
(*Setting tea-cloth*)

I like the sitting room. I can look onto the corner and see what's going on. And believe me, Herr Issyvoo, there is plenty. Those women—they are as old as I am—almost—and they stand there and whisper to all the men who pass by—Komm, Süsser. And believe me, Herr Issyvoo, they come. Sometimes I think I shall adopt that profession myself.

CHRIS

Can I rent the other room, Fräulein Schneider? What do you charge for it?

FRÄULEIN SCHNEIDER

I have charged twenty-eight marks when times were good.

CHRIS

I can't afford twenty-eight.

FRÄULEIN SCHNEIDER
(*Ruffling his hair*)

Ach, du armer Junger. But of course you can rent it. I will not have you leave. You rent it for twenty marks.

CHRIS

You're very sweet, Fräulein Schneider.

FRÄULEIN SCHNEIDER

Sweet? Ja. Once I was sweet. Sweet as a sugar cake. Now I am sweet like a fat old bun. And soon you make a great deal of money with your stories that you are always writing, and you take this room again, and everyone is happy once more.

CHRIS

I'll buy you a fur coat.

FRÄULEIN SCHNEIDER

And then I become one of the ladies. Only I will not go up and down the street. I sit at my window in my fur coat and call out, "Komm, Süsser." Komm to the third floor. And then I open the coat a little—just a little—and what do you think I have on underneath? Nothing! I have nothing on underneath. (*Bell rings*) Ach Gott, there is the bell. It will be your young lady.

CHRIS

You need not tell her that I am leaving this room.

FRÄULEIN SCHNEIDER
(*On her way out*)

But of course not, Herr Issyvoo. You can trust me perfectly. And I will bring you serviettes for your coffee. Most ladylike. Ladies appreciate these things.
(*She goes out.* CHRIS *starts to tidy the room.*)

FRÄULEIN SCHNEIDER'S VOICE
(*Off*)

Nein, nein, Herr Wendel. Sie können nicht hinein gehen. Herr Issyvoo erwartet heute eine Dame.

FRITZ'S VOICE

Aber ich muss mit ihm sprechen. Christopher. Christopher.

CHRIS
(*Going to door*)

Fritz.

FRITZ'S VOICE

Fräulein Schneider says I cannot come in. She says you expect a lady.

CHRIS

Yes, I do. But that's all right. Come in, Fritz. (FRITZ *enters. Young and dark.* FRÄULEIN SCHNEIDER *stands behind*) Do you want some coffee? One of my pupils is coming.

FRITZ

But yes, I would like some coffee. *Black* coffee.

CHRIS

Will you make enough for three, Fräulein Schneider?

FRÄULEIN SCHNEIDER

You are too good, Herr Issyvoo. You entertain whoever comes. No matter whoever.
(*She goes out.*)

FRITZ

I do not think your landlady likes me. And that is with me all right. Ultimately, I do not like her, too. In fact, I think the world is lousy.

CHRIS

Is business bad?

FRITZ

It is terrible. Lousy and terrible. Or I pull off a new deal in the next month, or I go as a gigolo.

CHRIS

Either—or. I'm sorry. That's just force of habit.

FRITZ

I am speaking a lousy English just now. Sally says maybe she will give me a few lessons.

CHRIS

Who is Sally?

FRITZ

She is a friend of mine. Eventually she is coming around
here this afternoon. I want that you should know each other.

CHRIS

Is she a girl friend of yours?

FRITZ

Not yet. But she is wonderful, Chris.

CHRIS

Who is she? What does she do?

FRITZ

She is an actress. She sings at the Lady Windermere. Hot
stuff, believe me. Ultimately she has a bit of French in her.
Her mother was French.

CHRIS

I wonder what Natalia will think of her. Natalia Landauer
is the pupil I am expecting.

FRITZ

Landauer? Of the big department store?

CHRIS

Her father owns it. It's the family business.

FRITZ

But they must be enormously wealthy.

CHRIS

Oh, yes, they're stinking rich.

FRITZ

And are you going to marry her?

CHRIS
(*Laughing*)

Me? No, of course not.

FRITZ

Do you not want her?

CHRIS

Not a bit. Except as a pupil.

FRITZ

Then if I should meet her and perhaps make a pass after her, you would not mind?

CHRIS

But you haven't even seen her.

FRITZ

Why would that make a difference? I tell you, Chris, I need money. Maybe then her father will take a liking from me, and give me a job in the business. If I marry her, a partnership, perhaps.

CHRIS

What makes you think she'd have you?

FRITZ

All women will have me if I want them.

CHRIS

Not Sally, apparently.

FRITZ

Sally has been too busy. With other men. But one day she
will be free, and then I will ultimately get my look in.

CHRIS
(*Teasing him*)

Perhaps *you* won't be free. Perhaps you will be all tied up
with Natalia.

FRITZ
(*Seriously*)

Yes, business must come first, ultimately. I suppose she is
a Jewess?

CHRIS

Oh, yes.

FRITZ

Well, there is always something. And you know, Chris, I
and very broad-minded.
(*Bell rings.*)

CHRIS

That will be Natalia.

FRITZ

How do I look, Chris? How is my hair? (*He gets out a
comb and mirror*) Um Gotteswillen . . . a gray hair. No,
that is too much. (*He pulls it out*) You see, Chris dear, I must
marry soon. You will help me to arrange the marriage settle-
ment?
(*Voices off.*)

SALLY'S VOICE

Herr Isherwood ist er zu Hause?

FRITZ

That is Sally. Chris, put on your coat.

CHRIS

Why?

FRITZ

She is a lady. Very elegant.

FRÄULEIN'S VOICE

He is not here. He is not to house.

SALLY'S VOICE

But he must be. He is expecting me. Isn't Herr Wendel here?

FRITZ

(*Going to the door while* CHRIS *gets his coat from the cupboard*)

Sally—liebling . . .

SALLY'S VOICE

Fritz, darling. The old lady said there was nobody here.

FRITZ

Come in.

(SALLY *comes in. She is young and attractive. She wears black silk with a small cape over her shoulders, and a page boy's cap stuck jauntily on one side of her head. Her fingernails are painted emerald green.* FRÄULEIN SCHNEIDER *stands again in the doorway*)

Sally, this is Christopher. Christopher, this is Sally. Sally Bowles.

CHRIS
How do you do?

SALLY
I'm terribly glad to meet you.

CHRIS
Make coffee for four, will you, Fräulein Schneider?

SALLY
Oh, not for me. I'm allergic to coffee. I come out in the most sinister spots if I drink it before dinner.

CHRIS
(*To* FRÄULEIN SCHNEIDER)
Just for three, then.
(FRÄULEIN SCHNEIDER *goes.*)

SALLY
I always have Prairie Oysters for breakfast. Don't you adore them? Eggs with Worcester Sauce all sort of wooshed up together. I simply live on them. Actually, I suppose I couldn't have a whiskey and soda, could I? I'm simply dead.

CHRIS
I'm afraid I haven't got any whiskey.

SALLY
I thought you were English.

CHRIS
I am. But I'm also poor.

SALLY

Oh, so am I. Terribly poor. But I always have whiskey. I mean, I think one must. Do you have anything? I mean, anything besides coffee?

CHRIS

I think I've got a little spot of gin.

SALLY

Dear old Mother's ruin. Gin will be wonderful. (CHRIS *gets gin out of cupboard*) Am I terribly late, Fritz darling?

FRITZ

No, you are beautifully on time.

SALLY

I thought I wasn't going to be able to come at all. I had a most frantic row with my landlady. Finally, I just said Pig, and swept out.

CHRIS

What would you like in this—or this in?

SALLY

Have you got anything?

CHRIS
(Helplessly)
No, I don't think I have.

SALLY

Then I'll just have it straight.

CHRIS

I'm afraid it will have to be in a tooth glass.

SALLY

That will be wonderful. Give me one of your marvelous cigarettes, Fritz darling. Do you ever smoke any of Fritz's cigarettes? They're absolutely devastating. I'm sure they're full of opium, or something. They always make me feel terribly sensual.

CHRIS
(*Handing her the glass*)

Here you are.

SALLY

Thank you so much. This looks wonderful.
(*Sips it*)
Oh, it is. It's got an extraordinary taste. Like peppermint.

CHRIS

Oh, I'm afraid I can't have washed out the glass properly. That must be toothpaste. I'm so sorry.

SALLY

I think it is wonderful. Have some, Fritz. Taste it. Perhaps we can all make a fortune selling mint-flavored gin.

FRITZ
(*Tasting*)

It is extremely interesting.

SALLY
(*To* CHRIS)

You have some, too.

CHRIS
(*Tasting*)

It really isn't bad.

FRITZ

What for was your row with your landlady?

SALLY

Oh, it was absolutely awful. You should have heard the things she called me. I mean—well, I suppose in a way I may be a bit of a tart. . . . I mean, in a nice way—but one doesn't like to be called that. Just because I brought a man home with me last night. And, anyway, I'm terribly in love with him.

FRITZ

Anyone I know?

SALLY

You'll never guess. Klaus.

FRITZ

Klaus? Your accompanist, Klaus?

SALLY

Yes. He was always just like part of the piano to me. And then last night he was absolutely astonishing. Just like a faun, or something. He made me feel like a most marvelous nymph, miles away from anywhere, in the middle of the forest. And then the landlady came in and made the most boring re-marks, so I simply can't go back. I shall have to find a new room.

(*To* CHRIS)

I don't suppose you know of any, do you?

CHRIS

A room?

SALLY

Something like this, perhaps. I suppose there aren't any more in this flat?

CHRIS

Well, there is this one.

FRITZ

Why, are you leaving?

CHRIS

I'm leaving this room. I can't afford it any more.

SALLY

Is it terribly expensive?

CHRIS

I pay fifty marks a month. That includes breakfast.

SALLY
(*Rising*)

But that's nothing. I pay eighty for mine. This is very nice. (*She looks around*) Is that your bed? Oh, I think that's sweet —all hidden away like that. (*She looks behind the curtains*) Oh, that's where you keep things.

CHRIS
(*Laughing*)

Only when I have visitors.

SALLY

You mean I could really have this? How soon?

CHRIS

As soon as you like. I've only got to move across the hall. It won't take me a minute. And I know Fräulein Schneider is very anxious to let it.

SALLY

What is she like? I mean, is she going to make trouble if I bring men home occasionally? I mean, it would only be very occasionally, because I do think one ought to go to the man's rooms, if one can. I mean, it doesn't look so much as if one was sort of expecting it. And men feel very keenly about that sort of thing. And it won't be men, anyway. It'll only be Klaus. I've decided to be absolutely faithful to him. I really have. She wouldn't mind that, would she, or would she?

CHRIS

If she can let the room, I'm sure she wouldn't mind anything.

SALLY

I say, am I shocking you, talking like this?

CHRIS

Not a bit. No one ever shocks me when they try to.

SALLY

(*Rather sharply*)
Why do you say I'm trying to shock you?

CHRIS

I have an idea you like to try and shock everyone. Why do you paint your fingernails green?

SALLY

I think it's pretty. Don't you?

CHRIS

Suppose you thought it was pretty to paint dirty pictures on them, would you do that, too?

SALLY

Yes. You know, that's rather a good idea. Not dirty pictures exactly, but sort of *stimulating* ones. I must get someone to do it for me. Is he really unshockable, Fritz, or is he just pretending?

FRITZ

Oh, no. Chris is quite unshockable. I have tried many times, but ultimately I cannot do it.

CHRIS

But—there is a young lady coming this afternoon who *is* shockable. So would you mind awfully being just a bit more careful what you say? She's one of my pupils, and I do rather need her.

SALLY

Oh, but darling, of course. I'll be terribly ladylike.

CHRIS

And don't let her know I'm going to move out of here, do you mind? She'd probably start cutting down on my terms.

SALLY

I won't breathe a word.
(*Bell rings.*)

CHRIS

That must be her now.

SALLY

You'd better put the gin away.

CHRIS

Oh, yes, thanks.

SALLY

I'm afraid there isn't time for me to clean my nails. I'll try and keep my fists clenched.

NATALIA'S VOICE

Herr Isherwood?

FRÄULEIN SCHNEIDER'S VOICE

Ja, gnädiges Fräulein. Er erwartet Sie. Bitte sehr.
(*She opens the door and ushers in* NATALIA.)

FRÄULEIN SCHNEIDER

Bitte. Hier ist die Dame die sie erwartet haben, Herr Issyvoo.
(*She goes.* NATALIA *is about twenty-two—correctly dressed, very German, formal and decided.*)

CHRIS

Natalia. These are friends of mine. Miss Bowles, Fräulein Landauer, and Mr. Wendel. Fräulein Landauer.

FRITZ

Sehr erfreut, gnädiges Fräulein.

CHRIS

I think we'd better speak English. Fräulein Landauer speaks wonderful English.

FRITZ

I am charmed, dearest Miss.

(NATALIA *shakes hands with Sally, noticing her nails.*)

SALLY

(*Concealing them*)

How do you do?

NATALIA

I am well. I have just had a cold, but it is better now.

SALLY

(*Doing her best*)

Oh, I'm so sorry. Colds are beastly things, aren't they? One's head gets all stopped up.

NATALIA

This was a cold in the chest. It was not in my head. All the plegm was here.

(*She points to her chest.*)

SALLY

All the what?

NATALIA

The plegm that comes into the tubes.

CHRIS

Phlegm. You pronounce the "h."

NATALIA

Oh. Then why do you say phthisis—what the Lady of the Camellias had—and not pronounce the "h" there, too? (*A pause while she waits for an answer.*)

CHRIS

Well . . .

NATALIA

There must be a reason. You give it to me, please.

CHRIS

I don't know it. But you don't say p-tisis, either.

NATALIA

Then you should say "lem," and leave it right out as in thisis. I have lem in my chest. Is it not so? It is not an exact language, your English.

SALLY

What *is* phthisis?

NATALIA

It is consumption. From the lungs. They are consumed in phlegm.

SALLY

Do you mind not going on about it? I think I am going to be sick.
(FRÄULEIN SCHNEIDER *enters with the coffee, and then returns with a cake-stand and paper napkins.*)

NATALIA

But why should it make you sick? You do not have it.

SALLY

All stories about illness make me want to throw up. I saw a movie about syphilis the other night that was too awful. I couldn't let a man touch me for almost a week. Is it true you can get it from kissing?

FRITZ

Oh, yes—and your King, Henry the Eighth, caught it from letting Cardinal Wolsey whisper to him.

NATALIA

That is not, I think, founded in fact. But kissing, most decidedly yes. And from towels. And cups. I hope these have been cleaned properly.

CHRIS
(*Flippantly*)

Oh, yes. Fräulein Schneider always boils them every day.

SALLY

I mean, you can't ask every man to run out and have tests and things before you let him touch you. I mean, there isn't time, and he'd be off in a nip to someone much less particular.

(NATALIA *freezes.* CHRIS *comes in hastily.*)

CHRIS

Natalia, let me give you some coffee.

SALLY
(*Rising*)

Oh, Fräulein. Could I have a talk with your landlady, Chris darling?

CHRIS

There's plenty of time.

SALLY

Oh, we'll talk outside. Won't we, Fräulein darling? We'll have secrets together.
(*To* NATALIA)
If you'll excuse me.

NATALIA

But most obligingly.

SALLY
(*To* FRÄULEIN SCHNEIDER)
Komm, liebes Fräulein, wir werden haben Geheimnesse zusammen.
(*They go out together.*)

FRITZ
(*To* NATALIA, *while* FRITZ *passes coffee*)
You will allow me to pass you a cake, dearest Miss? They are jam tarts.

NATALIA

I thank you, no. I do not eat between meals. And Miss is not the correct way to address a lady in English. No sugar, neither. Just plain black coffee.

FRITZ

That, too, is how I like it. Black, black, black, like Othello.

NATALIA

You tell me, please, about Fräulein Bowles. She is a re-markable girl.

FRITZ

She is a night-club artist. Very talented.

NATALIA

Where does she perform?

FRITZ

At a club calling the Lady Windermere. You know perhaps the play from Oscar Villder, calling *Lady Windermere's
Fan*?

NATALIA
(*Correcting him*)
Called *Lady Windermere's Fan*. But of course I know it.
I have read it, both in English and in German. I think it is
better in German. But the club I do not know.

FRITZ

Would you let me take you to it one night, to hear Sally
sing?

CHRIS

Do you think it is quite the right place for Fräulein Landauer?

NATALIA

But why not?

CHRIS

Oh, I don't know. I just thought . . .

NATALIA

You thought what, please?

CHRIS

I don't know, really.

NATALIA

You don't know. Then I cannot help you.

CHRIS

I thought it might be just a bit—Bohemian.

NATALIA

Then I must see it. I accept your invitation, my dear sir.
When shall we go?

FRITZ

We could go tonight, if you are free.

NATALIA

I can be free. You will come and fetch me at a quarter to
nine.

FRITZ

Oh, but it doesn't start until after midnight. Sally never
goes on until one o'clock.

NATALIA

Then you fetch me please at a quarter to midnight. I will
give you my address. You will come, too, Christopher, and
we will be a party to hear your girl friend sing.

CHRIS

She is not my girl friend.

NATALIA

No? Then what is she, please?

CHRIS

She's—just a friend.

NATALIA

I see. And she is not a girl?

CHRIS

Yes, but . . .

NATALIA

Then why is she not a girl friend?

FRITZ

Girl friend means something more than a friend who is a girl, Fräulein.

NATALIA

So? What does it mean?

FRITZ

It means a sweetheart.

NATALIA

Ah, so. I did not know. Then I am not a girl friend of yours, Christopher?

CHRIS
(*Feebly*)

Unfortunately—no . . .

NATALIA

You do not mean that, Christopher. You say it only to be polite.

FRITZ

He ought to mean it.

NATALIA

(*Ever so slightly coquettish*)
You think, Herr Wendel?

FRITZ

I think very much.

NATALIA

And you too, are polite.

FRITZ

No, I am never polite. I am only sincere.
(SALLY *returns*.)

SALLY

It's all fixed up, Chris. The poor old thing was almost in
tears of gratitude.

NATALIA

And why was she so grateful?

SALLY

Because I'm moving in here.

CHRIS

(*Hurriedly*)
Sally! We are all coming to hear you sing tonight.

SALLY

Tonight? Oh, but, my dear, I shall be exhausted. I didn't
sleep a wink last night.

NATALIA

You had rather I come some other evening?

SALLY

Oh, I expect it will be all right. Only don't let the proprietor
bother you. He's quite a darling, really, but he takes dope
quite a lot, and sometimes it doesn't agree with him. He
pinches people. It doesn't mean anything.

NATALIA
(*Stiffly*)

I think now that I must go.

FRITZ

Please, if I may accompany you?

NATALIA

My dear young man, I am not sixty years old, and I can
go home unmolested all by myself.

CHRIS
(*Quoting*)

Bin weder Fräulein, weder schön, kann ungeleitet nach
Hause gehen.

SALLY

What is that?

NATALIA

It is from *Faust*.

CHRIS

It means, "I am not a virgin, and I am not beautiful, and
I can go home alone."

FRITZ
(*Earnestly*)
Oh, but that is not true. None of it is true. Not in this case.

SALLY
(*Eagerly*)
You mean you think Fräulein Landauer *is* a virgin? How
do you know?

NATALIA
You are filled with interesting curiosity, Fräulein Bowles,
but I must pull myself away. I say good-bye.

SALLY
Good-bye.

NATALIA
Good-bye, Christopher. I think I will talk to your landlady
on my way out. I do not like these rooms, and she is charg-
ing you too much.
(*She goes out with* FRITZ.)

SALLY
(*After a moment*)
I don't think that girl liked me very much, did she?

CHRIS
No, I don't think she really did.

SALLY
I'm sure I don't know why. I was doing my best. It won't
make any difference to you, will it? To your lessons, I mean?

CHRIS

No, I don't think so. She's very broad-minded in an intellectual sort of way. She'll probably decide it's her duty to understand you.

SALLY

What on earth was Fritz up to? I can't think what got into him, dancing about like that. He isn't after her, is he?

CHRIS

She's very rich, you know. And Fritz is very broke.

SALLY

Do you think he'll get anywhere with her?

CHRIS

I've always understood from him that women find him attractive.

SALLY

I shouldn't think *she* would, with his going on like that. I should think his best way with a girl of that kind would be to make a pounce.

CHRIS

I can't imagine anyone pouncing on Natalia.

SALLY

No, dear. That's why it would be so effective.

CHRIS

I believe you're right. You know, that's quite wonderful of you, Sally.

SALLY

It seems very simple to me. Give me the rest of that gin, will you, Chris? There's just a little left. Then you won't have to pack the bottle.

CHRIS
(*Getting it*)
Sure.

SALLY

And you're going to be right across the hall. I took a look at the room. It's not very nice. But you can use this any time you like, you know, and then if I'm low—or you are—we can just sob on each other's bosoms. I say, Fräulein Schneider's got a big one, hasn't she? Like an opera singer, or that woman in the music halls who can make hers jump. Can Fräulein Schneider do that?

CHRIS

We might train her.

SALLY
(*Looking at the paper on the table*)
Chapter One. Are you writing a novel?

CHRIS

Starting one.

SALLY
(*Reading*)
"I am a Camera, with its shutter open, quite passive." Do you mean this is a story written by a camera?

CHRIS
(*Laughing*)

No, it's written by me. I'm the camera.

SALLY

How do you mean?

CHRIS

I'm the one who sees it all. I don't take part. I don't really even think. I just sort of photograph it. Ask questions, maybe. How long have you been in Germany?

SALLY

About two months.

CHRIS

And your mother is French. (*She looks blank*) Fritz told me she was.

SALLY
(*Irritated*)

Fritz is an idiot. He's always inventing things. Mother's a bit County, but she's an absolute darling. I simply worship her. I'm afraid Daddy's side of the family comes out in me. You'd love Daddy. He doesn't care a damn for anyone. It was he who said I could go to London and learn acting. You see, I couldn't bear school, so I got myself expelled.

CHRIS

How did you do that?

SALLY

I told the headmistress I was going to have a baby.

CHRIS

Oh, rot, Sally, you didn't.

SALLY

Yes, I did. So they got a doctor to examine me, and then
when they found out there was nothing the matter they were
most frightfully disappointed. And the headmistress said that
a girl who could even think of anything so disgusting couldn't
possibly be let stay on. So I went to London. And that's where
things started happening.

CHRIS

What sort of things?

SALLY

Oh—things. I had a wonderful, voluptuous little room—
with no chairs—that's how I used to seduce men. One of them
told me I'd do better in Berlin. What do you think, Chris?

CHRIS

I think you're doing fine. I think you're wonderful, Sally.

SALLY

Do you, Chris dear? I think you're wonderful, too. We're
going to be real good friends, aren't we?

CHRIS

(*Rather slowly*)

Do you know, I believe we are. Real good friends.

SALLY

You know, Chris, you were quite right about my wanting
to shock people. I do, and I don't know why. I do think you
were clever to notice it. And, Chris, there's one thing more.

I'm not sure if you'll understand or not. I did tell Fritz my mother was French. I suppose I wanted to impress him.

CHRIS

What's so impressive about a French mother?

SALLY

I suppose it's like whores calling themselves French names to excite men. I'm a bit mad like that sometimes, Chris. You must be patient with me.

CHRIS

I will, Sally.

SALLY

And you'll swear on your honor not to tell Fritz? And if you do, I can cut your throat?

(Stands over him, mock-bullying him with a paper knife.)

CHRIS

From ear to ear. Sally, was that all true just now, what you told me about your family?

SALLY

Yes, of course it was. Well, most of it.

(Puts paper knife down)

Only, Chris, you mustn't ever ask me questions. If I want to tell you anything, I will. But I've got to be free.

CHRIS
(Amused)

Very well, Sally.

SALLY

I've got to have a free soul. You know, I think I'm really rather a strange and extraordinary person, Chris.

CHRIS

So do I, Sally.
  (*Copying her tone*)
Quite extraordinary.
  (*He starts to laugh. She joins in. Their laughter grows louder. She embraces him.*)

SALLY

Oh, Chris, you are awful.
  (*Releasing herself, she picks up her handbag and starts for the door*)
Look, darling, I must go. I'll be back in an hour with all my things, and you can help me unpack. So long, Chris.

CHRIS

So long, Sally.
  (*She leaves.*)

CHRIS

Well, I'd better start moving out of here. I bet Fräulein Schneider's pleased. Sally is just the kind of person she goes for. (*Takes two personal pictures from the wall and puts them on the table*) How do I know that? How do I know what kind of a person Sally is? I suppose that's what's so fascinating about her. People who talk like that about themselves *ought* to be lying. But I don't believe she is. And yet she's that mysterious thing my family calls a lady, too. (*Looks out of the window*) Look at her. She's even flirting with the taxi-driver. And she knows I'm watching her. Oh, my God. (*He laughs*) I've got to put that down right away. (*He sits at the desk and starts to write in a notebook*) Let's make notes. How would you describe her? Sally Bowles was a girl of about . . . I wonder how old she is. Her face is young, but her hands look terribly old. And they were dirty, too. Dirty as a little girl's hands. (*He writes again*) Sally's hands were like the old hands of a dirty little girl.

Curtain

ACT ONE

Scene II

Time: *About three months later.*

Scene: *The scene is very slightly changed. A few feminine touches. A doll or two. Some bottles and jars are spread out on the table. The Medici prints are missing, and a couple of other pictures, very sentimental, are in their places. A pair of silk stockings and a pair of panties on a hanger, drying. When the curtain rises,* FRÄULEIN SCHNEIDER *is tidying up the room. There is a knock on the door.*

FRÄULEIN SCHNEIDER

Ja, herein.
(CHRIS *enters.*)

CHRIS

Oh, is Sally not here?

FRÄULEIN SCHNEIDER

No, Herr Issyvoo, she has gone out. And so late she was getting up. It's not as if she were working nights any more. I don't think she is well, Herr Issyvoo.

CHRIS

Do you know where she keeps my thermometer, Fräulein Schneider? I want to take my temperature.

FRÄULEIN SCHNEIDER

What, again?

40

CHRIS

I've got pains in my back. I think I've got a slipped disk.

FRÄULEIN SCHNEIDER

I thought it was your stomach.

CHRIS

That was yesterday.

FRÄULEIN SCHNEIDER
(*Feeling his head*)
You have no temperature.

CHRIS

I'm not so sure. I'd like to see, if I can find the thermometer.

FRÄULEIN SCHNEIDER
(*Looking for it*)
I saw her using it only yesterday to stir those Prairie Oysters with. Ah, here it is. I think there is still a little egg on it, but it's on the case.

CHRIS

Thank you.
(*He opens thermometer and shakes it down*)
Has the afternoon post come yet?

FRÄULEIN SCHNEIDER

It will be here soon now. There was nothing for her this morning. (CHRIS *puts the thermometer in his mouth*) I begin to worry for Fräulein Sally. That friend Klaus of hers. Six weeks he has been away now in England and only one letter has he written. (*Bell rings*) There is the bell. (*She goes to answer it.*)

FRITZ'S VOICE

Ist Fräulein Bowles zu Hause?

FRÄULEIN SCHNEIDER

Nein, Herr Wendel. Aber Herr Issyvoo ist da. In ihren Zimmer. Gehen Sie nur hinein.
(FRITZ *enters.*)

FRITZ

Hello, Chris. Are you ill?

CHRIS

I don't know yet. Sit down.

FRITZ

What's the matter?

CHRIS

My legs don't seem to work properly.

FRITZ

That can be locomotor ataxia.

CHRIS

I know. That's what I'm afraid of.
(FRITZ *sits beside him, and tests his knee for reflex action. The first time nothing happens. They both look worried.* FRITZ *tries again, and* CHRIS's *leg reacts.*)

FRITZ
(*Pushing* CHRIS's *leg away*)

There is nothing the matter with you.

CHRIS
(*Removing the thermometer*)
I think it's just over normal.
(*Shakes thermometer down*)
I think I'll take some aspirin. How are you, Fritz? How's
Natalia?

FRITZ
Christopher, I cannot get anywhere with that girl. I have
spent money on her. Money I have not got. I meet her parents.
I write her poems. Poems from Heinrich Heine, and always
she recognizes them, and then she laughs at me. It is not even
the money any more. But when she will not let me make love
to her, it drives me ultimately mad. I kiss her, and it is like
my aunt. And, Chris, she has a wonderful body, and it is
untouched. By me or anybody.

CHRIS
Sally said you ought to pounce on her.

FRITZ
But no one could pounce on Natalia.

CHRIS
Sally said that's why it would be so effective. Knock her
down, or something. Throw her on a couch and ravish her.

FRITZ
You do not mean that, Chris.

CHRIS
You don't seem to be doing any good the usual way. How
do you ordinarily manage with women?

FRITZ

I have only to uncurl my little finger, and purr a little, and they come running. I think perhaps I try. I can after all do myself no harm. She is away now. I write to her every day. Now I will write no more. I wait for her to come home, and then I will pounce, and I will ravish, and I will snarl.

CHRIS

Good.

FRITZ

And what is with you, Chris? You still live in that dark, tiny prison of a room?

CHRIS

Oh, yes.

FRITZ

And can you get anyone else in the room at the same time?

CHRIS

Oh, yes. If they're fond of me.

FRITZ

Do you have any love-life now?

CHRIS

I have a little. Now and then.

FRITZ

And you will not talk about it. Not ever. You are so reticent. If Sally did not ultimately have a French mother, she would not talk about it, either.

CHRIS

A what? (*Remembering*) Oh . . . yes.

FRITZ

She is a strange girl. Half of her is so ultimately frank, and half is so sentimental.

(*He takes a picture from the wall*)

This picture. She has it with her everywhere. It is called "The Kitten's Awakening." It is childish.

(SALLY *enters. She is rather smarter than when we last saw her—a new and rather unsuitable hat. She carries several packages. She looks tired.*)

SALLY

Oh, hello, Chris. Hello, Fritz.

FRITZ

Hello, Sally. We were just admiring your picture.

SALLY

Oh, "The Kitten's Awakening." I've had that ever since I was a child. It's a dead kitten waking up in Heaven—with angel kittens around. Chris makes awful fun of it. But I think it's rather sweet.

FRITZ

It is very sweet.

SALLY

Goodness, it's hot out, and it's late September already.

CHRIS

You are very dressy today.

SALLY

I am? Oh, this hat. Yes, it's new.
(*She takes it off*)
Clive bought it for me. I don't like it much, but it cost so much money. Let's have a Prairie Oyster. Will you, Chris?

CHRIS

Not for me. I think they affect my legs.

SALLY

Fritz?

FRITZ

I would like to try one.

SALLY

I'll make them. Chris doesn't really know how.
(*She starts to do so, getting the eggs and things from under the washstand, and mixing them in two tooth glasses.*)

FRITZ

And who is this Clive who gives you hats?

SALLY

He's an American. Chris and I met him a week ago at the Troika bar. We were both sitting alone, having a beer each because we were both so bloody miserable, and he was sitting next to us, and he ordered champagne for us all, and we didn't separate till four the next morning. And ever since then we've hardly been apart, have we, Chris?

CHRIS

He's so rich, we daren't let him out of our sight.

FRITZ

And he is here just on vacation?

CHRIS

He lives on vacation. I've never seen anyone drink so much. He's unhappy, he says. But I've never really found out why. Have you, Sally?

SALLY

Yes, dear. It's his wives. There have been four of them, and they none of them liked him. And, before that, it was his peculiar grandfathers. They both raised him six months each. One was a Baptist, and the other lived in Paris. So, no wonder it split him! He's sort of lost faith in everything, and I think Chris and I are putting it back, in bits. That's why I feel all right about letting Clive give us things. There's a dozen pairs of silk stockings in there, Chris. And absolutely gallons of Chanel 5. Oh, and some shirts for you. Some silk shirts.

CHRIS

Good God.

SALLY

The colors are a bit outrageous, but they're the best silk. Where's something to stir this with? Oh, this pen will do. (*She picks up a fountain pen and stirs the Oysters*) There. (*She hands one over to* FRITZ, *who chokes over it. She gulps her own*) Oh, that's marvelous. I feel better already. How are you, Fritz? You know, Natalia came to see me several times, as though she were doing District Visiting and I were a fallen woman or something. But she seems to have stopped.

FRITZ

She is away with her parents. She comes back next week, and then there is a surprise for her. Chris has told me your advice—that I should pounce on her—and I am going to take it.

(*He takes another sip of his drink.*)

SALLY

What's the matter? Don't you like your Prairie Oyster?

FRITZ

It is a little painful. You drink them all down at once?

SALLY

Yes, they're better that way. Especially when you are not feeling well. They sort of come back at you.

CHRIS

Aren't you feeling well, Sally?

SALLY

Not really.

FRITZ

You would like me to go?

SALLY

Fritz darling—would you mind terribly? I would like to lie down a bit.

FRITZ

But of course. With me there are no compliments. Sally, you lie down. Then you feel better. I go now. You take her to dinner, Chris, and cheer her up.

CHRIS

I'll try. Good-bye, Fritz. (FRITZ *goes*) Sally, are you really feeling ill?

(*He gets her slippers, and helps her on with them.*)

SALLY

Not so much ill, as just wanting to get rid of him. Fritz is sweet. I mean, he's an old friend, but I thought if I had to go on being bright any longer that I'd die. I've got something to tell you, Chris.

CHRIS

What is it?

SALLY

Chris, I went to the doctor this afternoon, and—I'm going to have a baby.

CHRIS

Oh, my God!

SALLY

I've been afraid of it for a long time, only I wouldn't think about it. I kept pretending it wasn't true. Then yesterday I was sick, and then I fainted this morning. And that's what made me go.

CHRIS

Is it Klaus's child?

SALLY

Yes.

CHRIS

Does he know?

SALLY

(*Sharply*)

No, he doesn't.

CHRIS

Well, you're going to tell him, aren't you?

SALLY

I don't know. Chris, I haven't heard from him for weeks and weeks. I wrote to him last week, the nicest letter I could, and he hasn't answered. Not a word. You didn't like him, did you?

CHRIS

I didn't really know him. I didn't think he was good enough for you.

SALLY

That's sweet of you.

CHRIS

But you're going to tell him this, now?

SALLY

No. Not if he doesn't write to me. It's awful, Chris. I do want to marry him, and have a family. But I can't beg him. And that's what it would be like. I mean, I mayn't be up to much, but I do have some pride.

CHRIS

Well, what then—if he doesn't write?

SALLY

I don't know. That's what scares me. It's silly, Chris . . .
it happens to other girls. Almost all other girls. But I am
scared. Do you suppose they all are, too?

(*A knock at the door.*)

FRÄULEIN SCHNEIDER'S VOICE

It is I, Fräulein Sally. The post is here.

CHRIS
(*Sotto voce*)

She's been keeping an eye out for it.

SALLY

Come in.

FRÄULEIN SCHNEIDER
(*Entering*)

There is a letter for you. The one you want. From England.

SALLY

Oh, thank you.

FRÄULEIN SCHNEIDER

Ja, Fräulein.

(*She hands it to her, and waits.* SALLY *starts to undo her
packages.* FRÄULEIN SCHNEIDER *gives up and goes out.*
SALLY *waits for her to leave. Then she rips the letter
open.* CHRIS *stands by. She reads it. Her face changes.*)

CHRIS

What's the matter?

SALLY

It's what I thought. He's throwing me over.

CHRIS

Oh, no.

SALLY

Right over. With a whole lot of stuff about how badly he's behaved to me.

(*She hands* CHRIS *the first page. He reads it. She goes on with the second*)

Apparently there's someone else. An English girl. A Lady Gore-Eckersley. He says she is wonderful. She's a virgin. A Communist Virgin.

(*She lays the letter down*)

Well, those are two things no one could ever say of *me*.

CHRIS

(*Going to her, putting his arms around her*)

Oh, Sally, I'm sorry.

SALLY

(*Leaning against him*)

It's silly, isn't it?

CHRIS

It is a kind of bloody letter.

SALLY

I'm afraid he's rather a bloody person, really. Oh, Chris, I am a lousy picker. Always the duds who'll do me in.

CHRIS

I won't, Sally.

SALLY

I know. I suppose that's why I haven't been interested in you that way.

CHRIS

Sally, you'll have to tell Klaus. He'll have to help you.

SALLY

He'd only run away. Leave no address. Besides, it's just as much my fault as his.

CHRIS

Well, what are you going to do?

SALLY

I knew this was going to happen. I can't have the baby, Chris. It's awful because I want to. But not unless I'm married, and can look after it.

CHRIS
(*After a second*)

I'll marry you, Sally.

SALLY

Oh, Chris, what good would that do? Klaus's child—and I'd be a rotten sort of mother. Just a betrayed whore.

CHRIS
(*Sharply*)

Sally, for God's sake, stop calling yourself that. You know you're not.

SALLY
(*Bitterly*)

Yes, I am. Just that. A whore who's fallen in love with a swine, because he's her type, and then got caught. That's all. Just a whore and a fool.
(*She starts to cry.*)

CHRIS

Sally, stop crying.

SALLY

I've got to find someone.

CHRIS

Won't this doctor . . . ?

SALLY

No. He was quite shocked when I told him I wasn't married.

CHRIS

Then we'll get someone. Maybe we should ask Fräulein Schneider.

SALLY

Do you think *she'd* know anyone?

CHRIS

She knows just about everything, I've always thought. I'll call her. (*Opens door*) Fräulein Schneider. Fräulein. Can you come in here? (*He comes back*) It will be all right, Sally. I promise you.
(FRÄULEIN SCHNEIDER *enters.*)

FRÄULEIN SCHNEIDER

You called for me, Herr Issyvoo?

CHRIS

Yes. We need your advice. Do you want to tell her, Sally?

SALLY
(*Her back to them*)

No. You do it.

CHRIS

Well, you see, Fräulein Schneider, Sally is in a little bit of trouble . . .

FRÄULEIN SCHNEIDER

Ja?

CHRIS

She's going to have a baby.

FRÄULEIN SCHNEIDER

Um Gotteswillen.

CHRIS

So you see . . .

FRÄULEIN SCHNEIDER

But then this Herr Klaus, he will come back and marry her.

CHRIS

Well, you see, he isn't awfully anxious to. You see . . .

SALLY
(*Angrily*)

It isn't that at all, Chris. You never can tell anything right. It's I who doesn't want him, Fräulein. I don't ever want to see him again.

FRÄULEIN SCHNEIDER

Ach, so . . .

CHRIS

So you see, we want to get—er—to get rid of the baby. The point is—do you know anyone?

FRÄULEIN SCHNEIDER

Yes, I do. There was a young lady living here once, and she went to the doctor.

SALLY

For the same thing?

FRÄULEIN SCHNEIDER

Exactly the same thing.

SALLY

And was it all right?

FRÄULEIN SCHNEIDER

It was quite all right. I have his address and telephone number still. I kept it just in case it should ever happen again.

SALLY
(*Trying to be easy over it*)

I suppose it happens quite often, really?

FRÄULEIN SCHNEIDER

It can always happen. It is just bad luck.

SALLY

I'm glad you know someone.

FRÄULEIN SCHNEIDER

He is rather expensive. It is a certificate he has to give that your health will not let you have the risk of childbirth. It costs money, that certificate.

SALLY

How much?

FRÄULEIN SCHNEIDER

For this other young lady, it was three hundred marks.

CHRIS

Three hundred!

FRÄULEIN SCHNEIDER

We could make it a little cheaper, I think, if we argued. Maybe two hundred and fifty.

CHRIS

That's still an awful lot.

SALLY

I know it is. But I've got to do it, Chris. I really have. You'd better ring up the doctor, Fräulein, and see if he can see us.

FRÄULEIN SCHNEIDER

You like that I come with you?

SALLY

Oh, would you? That would be marvelous. Where—where does he do it?

FRÄULEIN SCHNEIDER

There is a nursing home. You stay there two or three days, and then you come back here and rest. In maybe ten days, no more, it is all forgotten. I go telephone.

(*She goes out, gaily.*)

SALLY

It's like a treat to *her*.

CHRIS

It'll be all right, Sally. I know it will. The other girl was all right.

SALLY

There's something so *degrading* about it, as well as dangerous. Oh, damn! Isn't it idiotic? All the men I've had—and there have been quite a lot—and this has to happen to me. It's awful, too, when you think about it—that there's something alive inside of you—that you can't have. That you mustn't have. It's like finding out that all the old rules are true, after all. But I've got to go through with it.

CHRIS

Sally, two hundred and fifty marks. And the home will probably cost a bit of money, too. I've started making a little more now, too. If I can help you . . .

SALLY

Oh, Chris, you are an angel. I'll pay you back. I swear I will. And you know, I think maybe you had better come with

us. We'll say you're the father. I think it looks better to have
him along.

CHRIS

Yes, Sally, of course I'll come with you.

SALLY

Oh, Chris, I don't know what I'd do without you.
(*He holds her. Bell rings*)
Oh, damn, there's the bell. If it's anyone for me, I'm not
home. I won't see anyone.
(*Opens the door, and goes down the passage*)
Fräulein Schneider, I'm not . . . Oh, hello, Clive.

CLIVE'S VOICE

Hello, there. I just thought I'd come and look you up.

SALLY
(*Returning*)

Yes, of course. Come in.
(CLIVE *enters. He is in his late thirties, large, American,
blond and drunkish.*)

CLIVE

Well, hello, Chris, you son of a gun.

CHRIS

Hello, Clive.

CLIVE
(*To Sally*)

I've never seen your place before. I thought I'd come and
take a gander at it. I brought you these.
(*He presents an enormous box of very expensive flowers.*)

SALLY

Oh, Clive, how wonderful of you. Look, Chris, from that terribly expensive shop on the Linden.

CHRIS

Goodness.

CLIVE

So this is where you live, eh? Just one room? Say, it's not very grand, is it? Can't you do better than this?

SALLY

I—er—I have in my time. This is just temporary.

CLIVE

Oh, sure. Sure.

CHRIS
(Defensive)

What's the matter with it?

CLIVE

Well, it's not exactly *de luxe,* do you think?

CHRIS
(*As before*)

I think it's fine.

CLIVE

Oh, sure. Sure. I wasn't casting any slurs. I just thought maybe something a bit larger. More modern. But it's okay. Say, I bet your rooms are bigger.

SALLY

Oh, yes, they're much bigger. They're wonderful.

CLIVE

Where are they?

CHRIS

Just across the hall.

CLIVE

Mind if I take a look?
(SALLY *starts to gesture wildly at* CHRIS *not to show his room.*)

CHRIS

Well—er—they're rather untidy just now.

CLIVE

That's all right with me.
(SALLY *repeats her gesture.*)

CHRIS

There are some things lying around that—well, that I wouldn't want anyone to see.

CLIVE

Say, what are those?

CHRIS

Just some personal things.

CLIVE

Boy, that's what I'd like to look at.

CHRIS

I'm awfully sorry, but I don't think . . .

CLIVE

You mean, you've got someone in there?

CHRIS

Well, er . . .

CLIVE

Why don't you come right out and say it, feller? Don't beat about the bush. Go on back to her. I'll understand.

CHRIS
(*Again on a gesture from* SALLY)
Well, she's—er—asleep just now.

CLIVE

And, boy, I bet she needs it. Well, say, now what have you got in the way of liquor?

SALLY

We've got some gin.

CHRIS

Not much.

SALLY

I'm afraid we're out of whiskey.

CLIVE

Say, you need some stores. I'll send you in a cellar. Now, look, what are we going to do? I've been all by myself all day, and it's driving me nuts. There's a place I've heard of out on the Wannsee. The Regina Palast Garten. I thought we might drive out there for dinner.

CLIVE

SALLY

The three of us.

CLIVE
(*To* CHRIS)

If you're free.
(SALLY *nods at* CHRIS.)

CHRIS

Oh, yes, I'll be free.

CLIVE

Is that a good place?

CHRIS

I've always heard it was.

CLIVE

But you've never been there?

CHRIS

It's much too expensive for us.

CLIVE

Well, fine. Only is it *really* a good place? Can we have a good time there? The real McCoy?

SALLY

It's about the best place there is.

CLIVE

Oh, well, swell, then. That's great. That's the *real* thing. Well, shall we go?

SALLY

I can't go yet.

CLIVE

Why, what have you got on?
(FRÄULEIN SCHNEIDER *enters.*)

FRÄULEIN SCHNEIDER

Fräulein Sally, can I speak to you a moment, please?

CLIVE

That's all right. You speak up. No secrets here. No secrets in front of Uncle Clive.

SALLY

Have you talked to the—to the man, Fräulein?

FRÄULEIN SCHNEIDER

He says he can see you right away.

SALLY

Oh—oh, thanks.

FRÄULEIN SCHNEIDER

It takes twenty minutes from here. I think maybe you should go now.

SALLY

Oh, yes, I will. You get your hat and coat, Fräulein, and I'll be ready.

FRÄULEIN SCHNEIDER

Ja, Fräulein.
(*She goes.*)

CLIVE

What man is this?

SALLY

It's just a man about a job. A sort of audition.

CLIVE

I'll drive you there.

SALLY

I don't think you'd better. I mean, it's not a very big job, and it would look a little funny if I were to arrive in a Dusenberg car.

CLIVE

It would make them pay you more.

SALLY

Look, Clive, it's awfully sweet of you, but I think we'd better go by bus.

CLIVE

You take your landlady on auditions with you?

SALLY

Sometimes. She gives me confidence.

CLIVE

Well, then, Chris and I will go to the Adlon, and sit in the bar and wait for you. He can bring his girl along, if he wants to.

CHRIS

Oh, no, that's all right. But—I've got to go out, too.

CLIVE

Not with Sally?

CHRIS

No, but I have to go—and then come back here for just a minute. Why don't we all meet later at the Adlon?

CLIVE

I'll send my car back here for you. Six o'clock?

SALLY

That would be wonderful. And thank you so much for these.

CLIVE

Well, good luck. I hope you get the job.

SALLY

I do, too. At least, I—I think I do.

CLIVE

We'll celebrate tonight, if you do. And if you don't, well, then, we'll tie a bun on anyway, just to forget it all. So either way, you can't lose. So long, Chris, you sexy old bastard. See you both later.

(*He goes.*)

SALLY

Oh, Chris, I thought we were never going to get rid of him.

CHRIS

Yes, so did I. You know, he is an extraordinary man.

SALLY

But he's awfully sweet, really. Perhaps when this is over, I can devote myself to him. I've always thought I'd like to have a really rich man for a lover. I wouldn't want more than three thousand a year—pounds, I mean—and a flat and a decent car. Or maybe I could marry him, and then I might reform him. I could, you know, I really could.

CHRIS

Sally, do you really think you could reform anyone?

SALLY

Oh, Chris, don't. Don't pull me down again. I feel awful.

CHRIS

I'm sorry, Sally. And don't worry about reforming people. You're sweet. You really are.

SALLY

Thank you, Chris. Even if you don't mean it.

CHRIS

But I do. And now we'd better get going.

SALLY

Yes, I suppose so. (CHRIS *helps* SALLY *on with her shoes*) I suppose we should put these flowers in water. They cost such a lot. I'll just put them in the bath for now. Then I'll see if Fräulein Schneider is ready, and come back for my hat. (*She goes to the door, and turns to* CHRIS) Thank you for offering to marry me.

(*She exits.*)

CHRIS

(*Her slippers in his hand*)

And this is the kind of thing we used to make dirty jokes about at school. The facts of life. And here we go to prove they're not true, or that you can duck them.

(*Drops the slippers*)

And then we'll get pounds and pounds spent on us for dinner. And drink too much. And try to believe that none of it matters anyway.

(*Gets a cigarette from his pocket*)

And soon, as Fräulein Schneider said, we'll forget the whole thing. It'll seem like another of those nasty dreams. And we won't believe or remember a thing about it. Either of us.

(*He starts to put the cigarette in his mouth. Then he stops, and looks at the door*)

Or will we?

Curtain

ACT TWO

ACT TWO

SCENE I

SCENE: *About a week later.* CHRIS *is alone, sitting on the ottoman pasting photographs in an album. The sofa has been moved to the window and the table to the center of the room. The large chair has been placed at the right of the table. There is another chair to the left of the table.*

CHRIS
(*Arranges some photographs, then stops*)
This awful, obscene laziness. I ought to be flogged. Where has the time gone to? Jittering helplessly over the bad news in the papers, staring half-drunk at my reflection in the mirrors of bars, skimming crime-novels, hunting for sex. This place stinks of my failure.
(SALLY *comes back into the room. She wears a robe and looks pale and ill.*)

CHRIS
Are you all right?

SALLY
Yes, I'm all right. Just. Goodness, if it takes all that effort, just to go across the hall.
(*Passing behind* CHRIS, *she ruffles his hair*)
How's all your locomotor ataxia, Chris?

CHRIS
Oh, that's gone. I must have imagined it. (*Feeling his left side*) But, you know, I think I've got appendicitis.

71

SALLY

(Settling down to a half-finished Solitaire)

If you have, you just die of it. Don't let them operate on you. You know, Chris, what I would really like would be some champagne. Some really cold champagne.

CHRIS

I'm afraid we haven't got any of that.

SALLY

Clive ought to have sent us whole baskets of it. I do think it was odd his disappearing like he did. Where do you think he went, Chris?

CHRIS

I wonder if he didn't go off on an opium jag.

SALLY

That's quite possible. I never thought of that. Oh dear, I've known a lot of opium fiends, and you never could really rely on them. And then what happens to my career?

CHRIS

Do you really think he's going to do anything about that?

SALLY

He says he's going to put up all the money for a show for me. All I've got to do now is find the show. And then find *him* again. But until he shows up we don't get any champagne, and I do want some. I want some terribly, now I've thought about it.

CHRIS

I'd buy you some, if I could, Sally. But you know we really are desperately broke.

SALLY

You know, Chris, in some ways now I wish I had had that kid. The last day or two, I've been sort of feeling what it would be like to be a mother. Do you know, last night I sat here for a long time by myself, and held this teddy-bear in my arms, and imagined it was my baby? I felt a most marvelous sort of shut-off feeling from all the rest of the world. I imagined how it would grow up, and how after I'd put it to bed at nights, I'd go out and make love to filthy old men to get money to pay for its clothes and food.

CHRIS

You mean, a baby would be your purpose in life?

SALLY

Yes, I wouldn't think of myself at all. Just it. It must be rather wonderful never to think of yourself, just of someone else. I suppose that's what people mean by religion. Do you think I could be a nun, Chris? I really rather think I could. All pale and pious, singing sort of faint and lovely hymns all day long.

CHRIS

I think you'd get tired of it. You'd better just marry and have a child.

SALLY

I feel as if I'd lost faith in men. Even you, Christopher, if you were to go out into the street now and be run over by a taxi . . . I should be sorry in a way, of course, but I shouldn't really care a damn.

CHRIS
(*Laughing*)

Thank you, Sally.

SALLY
(*Moving to him*)

I didn't mean that, of course, darling—at least, not per-
sonally. You mustn't mind what I say when I'm like this. I
can see now why people say operations like that are wrong.
They are. You know, the whole business of having children is
all wrong. It's a most wonderful thing, and it ought to be the
result of something very rare and special and sort of privileged,
instead of just *that*! What are you grinning about?

CHRIS

Well, that's what it's supposed to be. The result of something rare and special. That's what *that's* supposed to be.

SALLY

Oh, goodness, is it? Yes, I suppose it *is* supposed to be.
Oh, is *that* why people say it's wrong to do it when you're
not married, or terribly deeply in love?

CHRIS

Yes, of course it is.

SALLY

Well, why didn't anyone ever *tell* me?

CHRIS

I expect they did, and you didn't believe them.

SALLY

Did *you* believe them when they told you?

CHRIS

No, Sally.

SALLY

But you think they're right?

CHRIS

I suppose I do.

SALLY

Then why can't we do things that we know are right?

CHRIS

I don't know, Sally. But it seems we can't. Do you really think you're going to stop having sex just because of this? Forever?

SALLY

No, I don't suppose I do.

CHRIS

I don't think we'll ever quite trust things, in the long run.

SALLY

I trust you, Chris. I'm terribly fond of you.

CHRIS

I'm fond of you too, Sally.

SALLY

And you're not in love with me, are you?

CHRIS

No, I'm not in love with you.

SALLY

I'm awfully glad. I wanted you to like me from the first minute we met. But I'm glad you're not in love with me. Somehow or other, I couldn't possibly be in love with you. . . . So, if you had been, everything would have spoiled. Hold my hand, Chris, and let's swear eternal friendship.

CHRIS

(*Taking her hand*)

I swear eternal friendship.

SALLY

So do I.

(*The bell rings*)

Oh dear, I wonder who that is. I hope it's no one for us. Chris, suppose it was Klaus?

CHRIS

What would you do?

SALLY

I'd be very good and noble about it. I wouldn't tell him anything—about the child, or anything. I'd just forgive him, beautifully.

(FRÄULEIN SCHNEIDER *enters*.)

FRÄULEIN SCHNEIDER

It is Fräulein Landauer to see you, Fräulein.

(NATALIA *enters*.)

CHRIS

Hello, Natalia.

NATALIA

Fräulein Bowles, I am but just back from the country and
I have only just heard that you have not been well. So I have
hurried in to see you.

SALLY

That's very nice of you.

NATALIA

(*Turning*)

Oh, hello, Christopher.

CHRIS

Hello, Natalia.

NATALIA

(*To* SALLY)

I bring you these few flowers.

SALLY

Oh, thank you so much. Chris . . .
(*He takes them.*)

NATALIA

What is, please, that has been the matter with you?

CHRIS

(*Quickly*)

Oh, just a little ulcer, that's all. They had to cut it out.

NATALIA

Where was the ulcer?

SALLY

Inside.

NATALIA

But, of course, it was inside. Where, please, inside?

SALLY

I don't really know. In here, somewhere.

NATALIA

And who, please, was it who cut it out for you?

SALLY

The doctor.

NATALIA

But yes, it was the doctor. I did not think it was the sewing-lady. What doctor is it you go to?

SALLY

A doctor . . .
    (*She checks herself*)
I forget his name. What was it, Chris?

CHRIS

A Doctor—Mayer.

NATALIA

I do not know of him. All of my uncles are doctors. You should have gone to one of them. I will ask one of them to come and examine you.

SALLY

Oh, I'm quite all right again now. Would you like some coffee or anything?

NATALIA

Yes, I think that I would like some coffee.

SALLY

Will you get it, Chris?

NATALIA

And Christopher, if you could stay away for just a little while, it would be nice, too. I have something that I wish to say to Fräulein Bowles.

CHRIS

Yes, of course.
(*He goes out.*)

NATALIA

Tell me, Fräulein, please, have you seen Fritz Wendel lately?

SALLY

No, I haven't.

NATALIA

I come back from the country two days before yesterday. He comes to call on me that evening. Fräulein, I think I have done you perhaps an injustice.

SALLY

Oh?

NATALIA

I have always think of you as a young lady who has no control of herself, and I have been disdainful of you therefrom. I am sorry. I do not think I quite understood.

SALLY

How do you mean?

NATALIA

I have think always that I have control of myself. Please, you will not laugh at me if I tell you something that is very personal to me?

SALLY

No, of course I won't.

NATALIA

I do not know of anyone else to whom I can go for some advice. Fräulein Bowles, Fritz Wendel has made love to me, and I have not taken him seriously, because it is all too formal, too discreet. Then, two nights before last, it is all changed. He throws aside his formality, and it is quite different. I have never known a man like that. And it has disturbed me. I cannot sleep for it. And that is not like me.

SALLY

But what am I supposed to tell you?

NATALIA

I wish to know, please, if I should marry him. My parents tell me no. They care for me. They think only of me, and they do not care for him. And he is not Jewish, and they wish that I should marry a Jewish man. I have always wished so, myself. Now I do not care. Only I think perhaps there is something of Herr Wendel's life that I do not know, that perhaps you do. And that therefore I should not marry him. You will tell me, please?

SALLY

Yes, I . . . I think perhaps there is.

NATALIA

What, please?

SALLY

I . . . I don't think I can tell you, exactly. But I don't really think he's your kind. I don't really think you ought to marry him—not if you ask me like that, point-blank.

NATALIA

I do not think so, too. But I think if I do not, that perhaps I will kill myself.

SALLY

Oh, no, you won't.

NATALIA

I do not think you know me. I do not think I know myself. (*She begins to cry.*)

SALLY

Oh, there's nothing to cry about. (NATALIA *goes on*) Oh, don't. Please don't. You'll have me crying, too. I'm most frightfully weak still, and I cry over almost anything.

NATALIA

(*Still crying*)

I am sorry. I did not know that love was like this. It is not what the poets have said. It is awful, and it is degrading.

SALLY

Yes, I know. It is. It's absolutely awful when it really hits you. But you mustn't give in to it, really, you mustn't. I know that sounds silly coming from me. But what do you think has been the matter with me? I was going to have a baby, and the chap let me down, and I had to get rid of it.

NATALIA
(*Turning, amazed*)
Oh, I am sorry. I did not know.

SALLY

And marriage isn't going to make it any better if it's not the right man. And I really don't think Fritz is. For you.

NATALIA
You think, then, that I must be strong?

SALLY

Yes, I do.

NATALIA
I think so, too. But um Gotteswillen, what is there to *do* with one's life, all of a sudden?

SALLY
You could become a nun. Do they have Jewish nuns?
(CHRIS *taps on the door.*)

CHRIS'S VOICE
The coffee is all ready.

NATALIA

You may come in now.
(*She turns her back, and straightens her face.* CHRIS *comes in with coffee.*)

CHRIS

I only brought one cup. Sally doesn't take it, and I think I'm getting allergic to it, too.

NATALIA

You are very kind, but I do not think now that I have time.
(*She turns*)
So, Christopher, we will start our lessons again now? I think now that I will perhaps take more. I will take two every day. You can manage that?

CHRIS

Yes, I can manage it. But that is an awful lot for you. It's an awful lot to do.

NATALIA

I need an awful lot to do. Good-bye, Fräulein. I thank you, and I come again.
(*She goes out, rather hurriedly.*)

CHRIS

What was all that about?

SALLY

(*Very nobly and remotely*)
That was something personal. That poor girl is terribly unhappy.

CHRIS

What about?

SALLY
(*As before*)
This is something between women. (CHRIS *giggles*) It is. I've
given her some advice. Some very good advice.

CHRIS
You gave Fritz some advice, too.

SALLY
Oh, I did, didn't I? Oh, that was awful. Because it paid off.
I'm never going to be funny and flippant again. I'm going
to be dead serious, and take everyone's problems to heart. I
am, Chris. I wish you wouldn't sit there, and snigger like
that. You don't know how silly it makes you look.
(*Bell rings offstage.*)

CHRIS
I'm a bit on your nerves, aren't I, Sally?

SALLY
Yes, you are. Oh, it's not only you. It's everyone. I'm on my
own nerves.

FRÄULEIN SCHNEIDER
(*Opening door*)
Fräulein Sally, hier ist der Herr Americaner. Bitte, mein
Herr. Bitte sehr.
(CLIVE *comes in. He carries a basket of champagne.*)

CLIVE
Well, hello, hello, hello there.

SALLY
Well, hello, Clive.

CHRIS

Hello.

(*Handshakes are performed.*)

SALLY

We thought you'd forgotten all about us.

CLIVE

Oh, for God's sake, no. Say, I've only just heard you'd been sick. Why didn't you let me know?

SALLY

You weren't around.

CLIVE

What was the matter with you, anyway?

SALLY

I had an operation.

CLIVE

Oh gee, that's tough. How are you feeling now?

SALLY

Better. Much better. Now that I've seen you.

CLIVE

Well, that's fine. Feel like coming out to dinner tonight?

SALLY

I can't do that. It's all I can do to get to the bathroom.

CLIVE

Ah, come on. Do you good.

CHRIS

She can't, Clive. She really can't walk yet.

CLIVE

Oh, hell, anyone can walk if they want to.

CHRIS

No, she mustn't. Really.

CLIVE

Well, let's have dinner up here, then. All of us. I brought you some champagne.

SALLY

Oh, Clive, how wonderful of you. I was just saying to Chris that what I'd like best in the world would be some champagne.

CLIVE

Well, let's have it. It's still good and cold. I only just got it. Open it, will you, Chris, there's a good feller?

CHRIS

I'll just get another glass from my room.
(*He goes out.*)

CLIVE

Well, let's take a look at you. Gee, you're a pale little lady. We'll have to pack you off some place to perk you up a bit. Where would you like to go?

SALLY

I don't really know, Clive. I think maybe I ought to stay here for my career.

CLIVE
(Vaguely)

Your career?

SALLY

Yes, the theatre.

CLIVE

Oh, sure, sure.

SALLY

I mean, if I am going to do a play, we ought to start thinking and planning a bit quite soon.

CLIVE

Oh, plenty of time for that. Get you well first.
(CHRIS *returns with a tooth glass, and gets two more from the washstand.*)

SALLY

I'll be all right in a few days.

CLIVE

Get you really well.

SALLY

No, but Clive, I do think . . .

CLIVE

You leave that all to me. Leave that all to Uncle Clive. (*To* CHRIS) Say, are those the best glasses you can manage?

CHRIS

I think Fräulein Schneider may have some others.

SALLY

Don't bother, darling. All I want is the champagne. Open it, won't you?

CHRIS

All right.
      (*He starts to do so.*)

SALLY

Where have you been, Clive?

CLIVE

Been?

SALLY

You've been away somewhere, haven't you?

CLIVE

Ah, just for a day or two.

SALLY

It's ten days.

CLIVE

Is it? Yeah, it may have been. I can never keep track of time when I'm on a bat. You know, this is a funny city. Driving here, just now, we ran right into a bit of shooting.

CHRIS

Shooting?

CLIVE

Seemed just like Chicago.

SALLY

Who was shooting at whom?

CLIVE

I don't know. Just shooting. Couple of people in the street, I guess. I thought I saw a fellow lying there, and a lot of people running in the opposite direction.

CHRIS

Where was this?

CLIVE

I don't know. Right in front of one of the big department stores. Birnbaum's, I think, where we bought you those fancy undies.

CHRIS

That's a Jewish store. That would be Nazi rioting, I imagine.

CLIVE

Say, who are these Nazis, anyway? I keep reading the word in the papers, when I look at them, and I never know who they are referring to. Are the Nazis the same as the Jews?

CHRIS

No—they're—well, they're more or less the opposite.
(*The champagne bottle is opened.*)

SALLY

Oh, that looks wonderful.

CLIVE

And there's a funeral going on today, too.

SALLY

Darling, isn't there always?

CLIVE

No, but this is the real thing. This is a real elegant funeral. It's been going on for over an hour. With banners and streamers, and God knows what all. I wonder who the guy was? He must have been a real swell.

CHRIS
(*Passing glasses*)

He was an old liberal leader. They put him in prison once for trying to stop the war. So now everybody loves him.

SALLY

Oh, this is marvelous. Just what the doctor ordered. Let's drink to Clive. Our best friend.

CHRIS

To Clive.
(*They drink.*)

CLIVE

Well, thank you both. I'll drink to the pair of you. Two real good playmates.
(*He does so.*)

SALLY

You know, I think there's something almost sacred about champagne. The taste and the look of it. Like holy wine, or something. I think it's absolutely right that it's as expensive as it is. It makes one appreciate it more, like something really special. Like . . .

CHRIS

Like—*that*!

SALLY

Yes, exactly like *that*.

CLIVE

What's *that*?

SALLY
(*Vaguely noble*)
Oh—love, and that sort of thing.

CLIVE

You know, kids, this is a pretty dreary sort of town. I've been here three weeks, and I'm getting kind of fed up with it.

SALLY
(*Alarmed*)
You're not going away?

CLIVE

I was kinda thinking of it.

SALLY

Oh, no, Clive. You mustn't.

CLIVE
(*Suddenly*)
What do you say we *all* go? All three of us.

CHRIS

But where?

CLIVE

Where would you like to go?

CHRIS

(*As in a game*)

Anywhere in the world?

CLIVE

Anywhere in the world.

CHRIS

I think I'd like to go to India.

SALLY

Oh no, it's all so terribly unsanitary. I want to go somewhere terrifically mysterious and sinister, and full of history. I'd like to go to Egypt.

CLIVE

We can do both. Say, what do you say—we take off from here as soon as Sally's well enough? Take the Orient Express.

SALLY

That's such a lovely name.

CLIVE

Take it as far as Athens. Then we can fly to Egypt. Then back to Marseilles. From there we can get a boat to South America. Then Tahiti. Singapore. Japan.

CHRIS

You know, you manage to say those names as though they were stations on the subway.

SALLY

Well, he's been to them all heaps of times, haven't you, Clive darling?

CLIVE

Sure. Sure, I have. But I'd kind of get a kick out of showing them to you two kids. And then we can end up in California.

CHRIS

You don't mean it, do you, Clive? Just take off and go—just like that?

SALLY

But of course, Chris. Why ever not? This is sheer absolute heaven.

CHRIS

And what happens to your stage career?

SALLY

Oh, that can wait. Or we can pick it up again in California. I'm sure Clive knows all the movie magnates, don't you, Clive?

CLIVE

I know quite a few of them.

SALLY

I mean, you could get me on the films like that, if you wanted to?

CLIVE

Oh, I guess so. Well, what about it? When shall we take off? You won't need more than a week, will you? You can rest on the train.

SALLY

I can rest anywhere.

CLIVE

How's about a week from today?

SALLY

I think it would be marvelous.

CLIVE
(*To* CHRIS)

All right with you?

CHRIS
(*Sitting down, helplessly*)

Yes, I—I guess so.

CLIVE

Okay, that's that, then. And, look, if we're going to have dinner up here, I'd better go get us a few things. What would you like? Some caviar, to start with?

SALLY

Oh, I'd adore that.

CLIVE

Then some soup. Some green turtle, maybe. And a partridge. With salad, of course. And I guess some of that chestnut ice cream with whipped cream all over it. And some fruit—some peaches.

SALLY

Get something for Fräulein Schneider.

CHRIS

Get her a pineapple. It's her idea of real luxury.

CLIVE

I think maybe we'd better get some new china, too, and some decent glasses.

CHRIS

Well, if we're going away next week . . .

CLIVE

Oh heck, you can present them to your landlady to make up for your rent. I'll go get them.

SALLY

Why don't you send your driver?

CLIVE

Heck no, this is kinda fun. Something to do. I'll be right back. I'll get some real good brandy, too—half a dozen bottles —and we'll make a real picnic of it. So long, kids.
(*He goes out. A long silence.*)

SALLY

Isn't life extraordinary? Just when you think you've really touched bottom, something always turns up.

CHRIS

Do you think he means it?

SALLY

Yes, of course he does. You know, Chris, I really do adore him. I mean that. I really do.

CHRIS

I know. I've watched you doing it.

SALLY

You're looking all stunned. What's the matter?

CHRIS

I feel stunned. Doesn't it stun you when someone comes along and just whirls you right out of the whole flux of your life?

SALLY

No, dear, not a bit. Besides, my life hasn't got a flux. And I don't think yours has, either.

CHRIS

No, you're right, it hasn't.

SALLY

Well, then?

CHRIS

But what will become of us?

SALLY

We shall have a wonderful time.

CHRIS

And then?

SALLY

I don't know. Oh, stop bothering with it, Chris. You always spoil things so.

CHRIS

We shall never come back.

SALLY

I don't want to come back.

CHRIS

I suppose you'll marry him.

SALLY

Of course I will.

CHRIS

And I? What will I be?

SALLY

You'll be a sort of private secretary, or something.

CHRIS

Without any duties. You know, Sally, I can suddenly see myself ten years from now—in flannels and black-and-white shoes, pouring out drinks in the lounge of a Californian hotel. I'll be a bit glassy in the eyes, and a lot heavier round the jowls.

SALLY
You'll have to take a lot of exercise, that's all.

CHRIS
(*Going to the window*)
You were both quite right. We've got nothing to do with these Germans down there—or the shooting, or the funeral, with the dead man in his coffin, or the words on the banners. You know, in a few days, we shall have forfeited all kinship with about ninety-nine per cent of the world's population. The men and women who earn their livings, and insure their lives, and are anxious about the future of their children.

SALLY
It's the only way to live. Isn't there something in the Bible about "Take no thought for the morrow"? That's exactly what it means.

CHRIS
I think in the Middle Ages, people must have felt like this when they believed they had sold themselves to the devil.

SALLY
Well, you needn't come, if you don't want to.

CHRIS
Oh no, I shall come. It's a funny feeling. Sort of exhilarating. Not really unpleasant. And yet, I'm sort of scared, too. If I do this, I'm lost. And yet I'm going to do it.

SALLY
Darling, is there any more in that bottle of champagne?

CHRIS

Sure.

SALLY

(*Pouring*)

Chris, this is the end of one life, and the beginning of another. Two weeks from now, we'll probably be floating down the Nile, with the desert all round us in the moonlight, and all those marvelous sensual Arabs watching us from the tops of the pyramids. And then there'll be India. And a Maharajah will offer me my weight in diamonds if I'll spend one night in his harem.

CHRIS

You'd better put on some weight. Will you do it?

SALLY

Well, not unless he's one of the kind who looks like a sort of mixture of Valentino and Buddha. If you know what I mean.

CHRIS

Well, not exactly. What will I be doing all this time?

SALLY

Oh, you'll be looking simply marvelous and sexy in jodhpurs and an explorer's hat. And then there'll be feasts on volcanoes in the South Seas, and cocktails with Garbo. (*She pours more drinks*) Chris, what is it they say in German when you're going on a journey, and they want to wish you luck?

CHRIS

Hals and Beinbruch.

SALLY

What does that mean?

CHRIS

Neck and leg-break. It's supposed to stop you having them.

SALLY

That's wonderful.
    (*Raising her glass*)
Neck and leg-break, Chris.

CHRIS

Neck and leg-break.
    (*They drink.*)

Curtain

ACT TWO

Scene II

Scene: *Five days later. When the curtain rises,* CHRIS *is seated at the table finishing some coffee. There are one or two dress boxes lying around, and an open suitcase in front of the bed.*

(FRÄULEIN SCHNEIDER *enters, carrying a large package.*)

FRÄULEIN SCHNEIDER
Herr Issyvoo, there is a box for you from Landauer's store. I bring it in here, because the man has not come yet to repair the ceiling in your room. I think perhaps it is the news that has stopped him.

CHRIS
What news?

FRÄULEIN SCHNEIDER
They have closed the National Bank. I heard it this morning, and I couldn't believe it. I went down to see. And, Herr Issyvoo, it is true. The bank is closed at the corner of the Nollendorf Platz. There will be thousands ruined, I shouldn't wonder. Such times we live in! It was bad during the war. Then they promise us it will be better. And now it is almost worse again. It is the Jews. I know it is the Jews.

CHRIS
Fräulein Schneider, how can it be? You don't know what you are saying.

101

FRÄULEIN SCHNEIDER

They are too clever. And you buy things at Landauer's store. That is a Jewish store. What did you buy?

CHRIS
(*Opening the parcel*)
I bought a suit. It's—it's a tropical suit.
(*Then, with determination*)
Fräulein Schneider, there is something that I have got to tell you. I should have told you before. Fräulein Sally and I are going away. We're going—well, right round the world. We're leaving on Thursday.

FRÄULEIN SCHNEIDER

This Thursday? The day after tomorrow?

CHRIS

Yes, I'm afraid so. We'll pay you till the end of the month, of course.

FRÄULEIN SCHNEIDER

But, Herr Issyvoo, this is dreadful. Both of you going away, and my other rooms empty, too. And now with the banks closing—what shall I do?

CHRIS

I'm terribly sorry, but there are other tenants. There must be.

FRÄULEIN SCHNEIDER

How shall I live? And you tell me now, at the last minute!

CHRIS

I know. I'm sorry, but—you can have all that new china and glass we have.

FRÄULEIN SCHNEIDER
(*In an outburst*)

Never, never did I think it would come to this. To live on other people—to become fond of them, as I have on you. To help Fräulein Sally, take her to the doctor—and then to have you walk out like this, as though I were nothing but a landlady to whom you can fling the rent.

CHRIS
(*Helplessly*)

Fräulein Schneider, it's not that. . . .

FRÄULEIN SCHNEIDER

And now I am an old woman, and nobody will care what becomes of me. I can go drown myself in the Spree.
(*She is crying now.*)
(CHRIS *touches her.*)

CHRIS

Oh, please, Fräulein Schneider . . .

FRÄULEIN SCHNEIDER
(*Springing up*)

No, do not touch me. It is the Judas touch.
(SALLY *comes in. She wears a new, light suit, carries another dress box. She is very gay.*)

SALLY

What on earth's going on?

CHRIS

I've just broken it to Fräulein Schneider that we're leaving. I am afraid that she is rather upset.

FRÄULEIN SCHNEIDER

Upset? Yes, I am upset. You go off on a trip of the whole world. You can afford to do that. But me, I have had to wait for my money, because you were too hard up sometimes to pay me. And now you throw me the china and the glass as a tip. The china and the glass . . . I will throw them from the windows after your taxi as you go away. That is what I think from your china and your glass. And from you, too.

(*She goes out.*)

SALLY

You're quite right, Chris. She *is* upset. What did you have to tell her for?

CHRIS

Well, I thought we had to. It's only two days now. You know, that was sort of awful what she said, about our being able to afford this trip.

SALLY

I don't see why.

CHRIS

It doesn't seem wrong to you—to let Clive pay it all?

SALLY

Well, we couldn't do it, if he didn't. And he *wants* to. I mean, we didn't *ask* for it.

(*The bell rings.*)

CHRIS

I didn't feel that I could quite explain that to Fräulein Schneider.

SALLY

I've got an absolutely exquisite negligee. I must show it to you.

(She opens the box, and takes out a fluffy pink negligee)
Look, isn't it simply marvelous?

CHRIS

But, Sally, what are you going to need that for?

SALLY

Darling, to lie around in.

CHRIS

Where?

SALLY

Anywhere. I expect we'll do lots of lying around.
(FRÄULEIN SCHNEIDER, quite grim now, announces.)

FRÄULEIN SCHNEIDER

Herr Wendel.
(FRITZ enters. FRÄULEIN SCHNEIDER retires.)

FRITZ

Well, then, hello, you.

SALLY

Hello. Look, Fritz, don't you think this is wonderful?
(She shows the negligee, jumping on the ottoman to do so.)

FRITZ

But, yes. That is extremely seductive. It is for a part in the movies?

SALLY

No, it's to wear. We're going away, Fritz. Clive is taking
us. All around the world. We're leaving on Thursday.

FRITZ

You say again, please.

CHRIS

We're going round the world.

FRITZ

The two of you. (*They nod*) With Clive?

CHRIS

I know, Fritz. It doesn't sound likely. But he did ask us.

SALLY

Chris, do we have any of that champagne left?

CHRIS

Oh, yes, there are still about four bottles. You know he
brought a dozen.

SALLY

Let's open one.

CHRIS
(*Getting it*)

It isn't cold.

SALLY

That's all right. I'm terribly thirsty, and we've just got time
before his car arrives to fetch us to lunch.
    (CHRIS *gets a bottle and glasses from the washstand*)
How are you, Fritz?

FRITZ

I am not good. I am not good at all.

SALLY

Oh, dear, what's the trouble now?

FRITZ

I would like to tell you. Can I, please?

SALLY

Yes, of course.

FRITZ

You remember, Chris, the advice you give me from Natalia. I attempt it. I think it goes well. And then I go again to see her, and she sends me a note. She will not see me, she will never see me again.

(SALLY *turns away in embarrassment*)

I beg. I plead. I go again. At last she see me. She tell me it is all over. (CHRIS *opens the bottle and pours*) And she shows me a note that her father has received.

SALLY

From whom?

FRITZ

It is not signed. But it say, Herr Landauer, beware. We are going to settle the score with all you dirty Jews. We give you twenty-four hours to leave Germany. If not, you are dead men.

CHRIS
(*Stopping pouring*)

Good God! When was this?

FRITZ

This was last night. And she say that with that sort of thing she cannot think now from anything else, and I am to go away and never come back. And when I try to comfort her, and tell her that it is some silly schoolboy who writes it, she scream at me that I do not understand. That I am like all the others. That her father is worried sick, and her mother is falling all the time ohnmächtig . . .

SALLY

What is that?

CHRIS

Fainting.

FRITZ

Ja, she is falling fainting, and now will I go, please. Please. Please. Please. So I go.

SALLY
(*Embarrassed*)

Well . . . Chris, isn't that champagne ready yet?

CHRIS
(*Roused*)

Oh, yes.

SALLY

Well, let's have it. Here, Fritz. Here's how.

CHRIS

How.

FRITZ
(*Sadly*)
How.

SALLY
Oh, this is wonderful. Even warm, it is wonderful.

CHRIS
What is Herr Landauer going to do?

SALLY
I should think he is going away, isn't he?

FRITZ
No, he will not go away. He wants that Natalia and her
mother should go. And Natalia will not. I think her mother
will go to Paris. But Natalia will stay by her father.

SALLY
If it was me, I'd fly like a bird. If I could afford it. And I'm
sure they can. I mean, what is the point of staying, with that
sort of thing going on?

FRITZ
I do not know.
        (*He drinks again, then suddenly flings his glass from
        him with a melodramatic gesture*)
Verfluchter Kerl!
        (*He buries his head in his hands.*)

SALLY
Fritz, what on earth's the matter?

CHRIS

What is it?

FRITZ

It is I. Please, can I tell you something else? Can I tell you both something?

SALLY

Yes, of course.

FRITZ

It is something I have never told anyone in my life before. But now I must make confession. I am a Jew.

SALLY
(*Quite unperturbed*)

Well?

FRITZ

That does not surprise you?

SALLY

I sort of had an idea you were, especially when you made so much fuss about not being. And then I forgot all about it. But so what?

FRITZ

So what? I have lied and pretended. Even to Natalia I have lied.

CHRIS

If you were so keen on getting her, I should have thought that was the very thing to tell her.

SALLY

Her parents wanted her to marry a Jew.

FRITZ

I know. I know. She has told me that. And still I could not say it. I think I wanted it even more, that no one should ever know. Even now, I cannot be one from the Landauers, and have letters like that written to me. I am ashamed from myself, but it is so. And now I have told you, and now you know me for what I am. And it is not nice. It is not nice at all.

(*A long pause*)

Well, you say something, please.

SALLY

Fritz, I think you are taking it all too seriously. I mean, it is your own business.

FRITZ

I do not think it is any more. But still I cannot speak.

(*Bell rings.*)

SALLY

That'll be the car. Clive's car. Quick, let's have another drop of champagne. Fritz?

FRITZ

No, I do not want any more.

SALLY

Come on, it'll do you good. Here . . .

(*She offers him her glass. He pushes it away*)

Oh, well, have it your own way.

CHRIS
(*Touching* FRITZ)

Fritz, I am terribly sorry. (FRÄULEIN SCHNEIDER *enters with a note. She gives it to* SALLY *and goes out again*) I know it's not for me to give you any advice. I don't think I could, anyhow. But don't you think maybe you should tell Natalia that . . .

SALLY
(*Who has opened the note and read it*)

But . . . but . . .
(*She cannot speak.*)

CHRIS

What is it, Sally?

SALLY

Oh, it's nothing. Look, Fritz, we've got to go out to lunch . . .

CHRIS
(*Shocked*)

But, Sally . . .

SALLY
(*Sharply*)

Well, we have. And right away. Fritz, I'm not trying to get rid of you, but we do have to go.

FRITZ

Ja. Ja, of course.

SALLY

I'm most terribly sorry. And please, please come back. Come back soon.

FRITZ

But you are going away.

SALLY

Oh . . . yes . . . Well, come tomorrow.

FRITZ

I will see. Good-bye, Sally. Good-bye, Chris. I think maybe now I go pray a little. But in what church? I do not know.
(He goes out.)

CHRIS

Really, Sally, that was a little cruel. Fritz really is in trouble . . .

SALLY

Yes, well, so are we. Real trouble. Read that.
(She hands him the note. He reads it.)

CHRIS

Good God!

SALLY

Read it aloud, will you? I want to be sure I got it right.

CHRIS

(Reading)

"Dear Sally and Chris, I can't stick this damned town any longer. I'm off to the States. Hoping to see you sometime. Clive. These are in case I forgot anything." *(He looks in the envelope)* Three hundred marks. *(A long pause)* Well!

SALLY

I should think you might be able to say something better than "well."

CHRIS

I said "well" when it happened. I can't think of anything else to say, now it isn't going to.

SALLY

Do you think it's true?

CHRIS

Do you want to call up the hotel and see? See if he's gone?

SALLY

You call. I don't want him to think I'm running after him.

CHRIS

I feel rather the same way.

SALLY

We could ask Fräulein Schneider to call.
    (*Opens door*)
Fräulein Schneider . . . Fräulein Schneider . . .

CHRIS

What are you going to tell her?

SALLY

Nothing. Just ask her to call.

CHRIS

And if he's gone . . . ?

SALLY

Well, we should have to tell her in the end. That just shows why you shouldn't have told her now.

(FRÄULEIN SCHNEIDER *enters.*)

FRÄULEIN SCHNEIDER

You called for me?

SALLY

(*Over-sweetly*)

Yes, Schneiderschen. Will you be a liebling, and call the Adlon Hotel, and ask for Mr. Mortimer?

FRÄULEIN SCHNEIDER

You want to speak to him?

SALLY

No, I don't. I just want you to ask for him. And if he *is* there—well, say we'll be a little late for lunch. And then come and tell us.

(FRÄULEIN SCHNEIDER *goes without a word.*)

CHRIS

You know he's gone, don't you?

SALLY

I suppose I do, really. But we've got to be sure. Do you think he did it on purpose? Just to get us all steamed up, and then let us down like this?

CHRIS

I think he just got fed up.

SALLY

And what about us?

CHRIS

I don't imagine he even remembered us—or not for more than a minute. I think that's the way he lives. And that he leaves every town and every set of acquaintances just that way.

SALLY

Easy come, easy go.

CHRIS

Yes.

SALLY

We were easy come, all right. But, Chris, don't you think it was outrageous? I mean, really outrageous?

CHRIS

Sally, I don't think we've got too much right to have an opinion anyway, about the whole thing.

SALLY

And what have we got out of it?

CHRIS

Not much. But it didn't last very long.

SALLY

I don't think we're much good as gold-diggers, are we, darling?

(*They begin to laugh.* FRÄULEIN SCHNEIDER *returns.*)

FRÄULEIN SCHNEIDER

Herr Mortimer has left, Fräulein. He has gone back to the United States.

SALLY

I see. Thank you.

CHRIS

And, Fräulein Schneider, we won't be going away—after all.

FRÄULEIN SCHNEIDER
(*Overjoyed*)
Ah, Herr Issyvoo, you mean that?

CHRIS

Yes, I do.

FRÄULEIN SCHNEIDER

Oh, but that is good. That is wonderful. Neither of you? Not Fräulein Sally, either?

SALLY

No, neither of us.

FRÄULEIN SCHNEIDER

Then, that is a miracle. Oh, but I am happy. I am happy.
(*She seizes* SALLY *by the waist, and starts to dance.*)

SALLY
(*Releasing herself*)
Yes, I'm sure you're happy, Fräulein. But not now, please. I'd like you to leave us alone.

FRÄULEIN SCHNEIDER
(*Repentant*)
But, of course. Forgive me, Fräulein Sally. I go now.
(*She leaves.*)

CHRIS
Do you want to come out and have some lunch?

SALLY
I don't think I could eat any.

CHRIS
I don't, either.

SALLY
Well, there we are. We've got three hundred marks.

CHRIS
What are you going to do with them?

SALLY
We'll divide them.

CHRIS
No, you take them. They were sent to you.

SALLY
They were meant for both of us. Halves, Chris.

CHRIS
Well, thank you.
(*She halves the money.*)

SALLY

I shall take this negligee back.

CHRIS

I'll take this suit back, too.

SALLY

(*Changing into mules and opening the jacket of her suit*)
And we shall have to find some work. There was a man
who wrote to me the other day about a job in Frankfurt. I
never answered him, because I thought we'd be gone. I'll go
and see him this afternoon. (*Starting to go through her address book*) He's a horrible old man, and he's always trying
to go to bed with me, but I've got to make some money,
somehow—I suppose. I've got his address here somewhere.

CHRIS

I'll have to put my advertisement in the paper again. English
lessons given.

SALLY

(*Finding something else*)
Oh, and there's this. Do you want to earn some money,
Chris?

CHRIS

You know I do. I need to.
       (*Puts suit box on floor.*)

SALLY

(*Pouring champagne*)
Well, there's a man who's starting a magazine. It's going
to be terribly highbrow with lots of marvelous modern photo-

graphs—you know, girls' heads reflected upside down in ink-pots.

(*Passing drinks*)

Here, Chris. It's silly to waste it. Well, he wanted me to write an article in the first number on the English girl. I forgot all about it, and I haven't an idea what to say, so why don't you do it for me? I'll give you the money.

CHRIS

That's fine. Thank you. But you must have part. How soon do you want it done?

SALLY

I should give it him in a day or two at the latest.

CHRIS

How long is it to be?

SALLY

Oh, I don't know. About *that long*. (*She gesticulates, then gets a book*) Here's a dictionary, in case there are any words you can't spell.

CHRIS
(*Taking it, amused*)

Good.

SALLY
(*Her arms around his neck*)

Oh, Chris, I do like you. You're like a marvelous brother.

CHRIS

I feel the same thing. But, you know, Sally, we've been delivered from something. From the Devil. I know it's disappointing, in a way. . . . That's where the old plays and operas were wrong. . . . There ought to be a sort of disappointment chorus at the end. But it is another chance.

SALLY

Yes, I know. It couldn't have gone on forever. Clive wasn't the type. He'd have ditched us somewhere, and that would have been far worse.

CHRIS

It would have been worse still if he hadn't ditched us.

SALLY

He never meant to play straight with us. You're right. He was the Devil.

CHRIS

I didn't mean that. The Devil was in *us*. Sally, how about our trying to reform, and change our way of life a bit?

SALLY

What's wrong with our way of life?

CHRIS

Just about everything. Isn't it?

SALLY

I suppose so. Not getting any work. Not even trying to. That operation. The lies I've written Mother. The way I haven't written her at all for weeks now.

CHRIS

Me, too. Can't we reform, Sally?

SALLY

Yes, we can. I'll tell you something, Chris. Something I've just decided.

CHRIS

What's that?

SALLY

I'm sick of being a whore. I'm never going to look at another man with money, as long as I live.
(*He laughs*)
What's funny about that?

CHRIS

Nothing. It's a beginning, anyway.

SALLY

What are *you* going to begin on?

CHRIS

I'm going to start work tomorrow morning.

SALLY
(*Carried away*)
We're both going to begin. We're going to be good. Oh, Chris, isn't it wonderful?

CHRIS
(*Smiling*)
Yes, Sally.

SALLY

We're going to be quite, quite different people. We're even going to look wonderful, too. People will turn around and stare at us in the street, because our eyes will be shining like diamonds.

CHRIS

Diamonds—without any rings under them.

SALLY
(*Very gaily*)
And think how we'll feel in the mornings. Imagine what it will be like to wake up without coughing, or feeling even the least little bit sick.

CHRIS

We'll have appetites like wolves. Ravening wolves.

SALLY

Don't you suppose we ought to diet? Eat just nuts and things?

CHRIS

All right. And we'll give up smoking in bed . . .

SALLY

And drinking before breakfast.

CHRIS
(*Shocked*)

Sally, do you?

SALLY

We must have a time-table. What time shall we get up?

CHRIS

Eight o'clock.

SALLY

Half-past seven.

CHRIS

All right.

SALLY

We shall take cold baths. You have yours first.

CHRIS

And do exercises.

SALLY

Then we'll have breakfast together, and talk German. Nothing but German.

CHRIS

Ja. Jawohl.

SALLY

Then we should study something. Do you think we could learn a useful trade?

CHRIS

We'll weave from eight-thirty to nine. And then spend an hour making small, hand-painted boxes.

SALLY
(*Laughing hard*)
And then it'll be time for you to start your novel, while I practice Interpretive Dancing. You know, with shawls and things . . .

CHRIS
Sally, joking aside. You are serious about all this, aren't you?

SALLY
Of course I am. Terribly serious.
(*She gets the address book*)
I'm going to start calling up everyone I know.

CHRIS
What for?

SALLY
To see what's going on. And then, one decent piece of luck . . .

CHRIS
(*Urgently*)
Oh, no, Sally. That isn't what we need. A piece of good luck today—a piece of bad luck tomorrow—always at the mercy of *things* again . . .

SALLY
One *is*. That's life. It's all accident.

CHRIS
(*As before*)
Accidents are only the result of things one's done. Things that one is.

SALLY

Why, I could go to a party tonight, and I could meet the most wonderful man, who'd make all the difference to my whole life and my career . . . (*She breaks off, looking at him*) What's the matter? Why do you look like that?

CHRIS
(*Slowly*)
Sally, you weren't serious. You didn't mean a word of it.

SALLY

Yes, I did. I meant every word. I'm going to be quite different. But there's no reason why I shouldn't go out. I don't have to shut myself up in prison. That isn't what you want, is it?

CHRIS
No, Sally, of course not. But . . .

SALLY
(*Angrily*)
Well, then, stop looking so disapproving. You're almost as bad as Mother. She never stopped nagging at me. That's why I had to lie to her. I always lie to people, or run away from them, if they won't accept me as I am.

CHRIS
I know you do, Sally.

SALLY
(*Putting on an act*)
I think I'm really rather a strange and extraordinary person, Chris.
(*Pause*)

What's the matter? You laughed at me the first time I told you that. Can't you laugh now? Come on.

(*She starts to laugh, not too brightly. He starts a moment later, still more feebly. The laughter dies. She tries again—it fails. They move slowly away from each other.*)

Curtain

ACT THREE

ACT THREE

Scene I

Scene: *Two days later. The room is untidy. A half-used coffee tray is on the table with a glass of brandy. The bed is unmade, and clothes are strewn around the room.* FRÄULEIN SCHNEIDER *is tidying up. There is a knock on the door.*

CHRIS'S VOICE

Sally, may I come in?

FRÄULEIN SCHNEIDER

Come in, Herr Issyvoo.
(CHRIS *comes in*)
Fräulein Sally is telephoning.

CHRIS

She's up very late.

FRÄULEIN SCHNEIDER

She was in very late last night.

CHRIS

I left a manuscript in here for her yesterday afternoon.

FRÄULEIN SCHNEIDER

She did not come back until almost six this morning. I think maybe she drank a little too much. Her clothes are all over

131

the floor. And she had only half her coffee this morning, and some brandy too. It is not good so early.

>   (SALLY *enters. She is wearing a robe, and looks hungover.*)

SALLY

Oh, hello, Chris.

CHRIS

Hello, Sally.

SALLY

Leave all that stuff for now, Fräulein. I'm going to wear it. I'm going out quite soon. You can do the room then.

FRÄULEIN SCHNEIDER

Very good, Fräulein.
>   (*She goes.*)

CHRIS

I haven't seen you for a day and a half.

SALLY

I know. I've missed you, Chris.

CHRIS

I've missed you, too. I say, you don't look too well this morning.

SALLY

I've got a terrible hangover.

CHRIS

What were you doing last night?

SALLY

I was out with some people. I've been out both nights. I've been an awful fool, Chris. But don't scold me, please.

CHRIS

What have you been up to?

SALLY

Oh, not *that*.

CHRIS

I wasn't thinking of that!

SALLY

But we never stopped going around. And then I got drunk and sentimental the first night, and I telephoned Mother in London.

CHRIS

Good God, what for?

SALLY

I suddenly felt like it. But we had the most awful connection, and I couldn't hear a word. And last night was worse. We went to the most boring places. Oh, Chris, I need someone to stop me. I really do. I wish I'd stayed home with you.

CHRIS

Well, thank you, Sally.

SALLY

But you're awfully nice to come back to.

CHRIS

You're nice to have come back. I say, that sounds like a popular song

SALLY

Oh, it does. Maybe we could write it together and make a fortune.
(*She improvises a tune*)
"You're awfully nice to come back to."

CHRIS
(*Doing the same*)
"You're awfully nice to come back."

SALLY AND CHRIS
(*Singing together*)
"You're awfully nice to come back to . . ."

SALLY
(*Her arms around him*)
I do think we belong together. Much more than if we'd ever had an affair. That little quarrel we had didn't mean anything, did it?

CHRIS

I don't think two people can live as close as we do, and not have them.

SALLY

But it was that that sent me out on that idiotic binge.

CHRIS
(*Pause*)
Did you read the article I left you?

SALLY

The what, dear?

CHRIS

My article.

SALLY
(*Vaguely*)
Oh, yes, I—looked at it.

CHRIS

Well?

SALLY
(*Too brightly*)
I'm terribly sorry, Chris. But it won't do.

CHRIS
Why, what's wrong with it?

SALLY

It's not nearly snappy enough.

CHRIS

Snappy?

SALLY

But it's all right, Christopher. I've got someone else to do it.

CHRIS

Oh? Who?

SALLY

Kurt Rosenthal. I called him this morning.

CHRIS

Who's he?

SALLY

Really, Chris, I thought you took an interest in the cinema.
He's miles the best young scenario writer. He earns pots of
money.

CHRIS

Then why's he doing this?

SALLY

As a favor to me. He said he'd dictate it while he's shaving,
and send it round to the editor's flat.

CHRIS

Well, journalism isn't really in my line. But I think you might have let me know.

SALLY

I didn't think you'd want to be bothered.

CHRIS

And *he* would?

SALLY
(*Starting to dress*)

He doesn't make such a fuss about writing as you do. He's writing a novel in his spare time. He's so terribly busy, he can only dictate it while he's having a bath.

CHRIS
(*Bitterly*)

I bet that makes it wonderful.

SALLY

He read me the first few chapters. Honestly, I think it's the best novel I've ever read.

CHRIS

But that doesn't add up to very many, does it?

SALLY
(*Her tone sharpening, from his*)

He's the kind of author I really admire. And he's not stuck up, either. Not like one of these young men who, because they've written one book, start talking about art, and imagining they're the most wonderful authors in the world.

CHRIS

Just who are you talking about, Sally?

SALLY
(*Brushing her hair*)
Well, you do, Chris. You know you do. And it's silly to get jealous.

CHRIS
(*Angrily*)
Jealous? Who's jealous?

SALLY

There's no need to get upset, either.

CHRIS
(*Furious*)
I am not upset. You don't like my article. All right, you needn't go on about it. I can't think why I expected you to, with that snappy little bird-brain of yours. Or your rich, successful friends either, from whom you seem to have got all this stuff about me.

SALLY
(*Equally angry*)
Would you like to know what my friends said about you?

CHRIS

No, I wouldn't.

SALLY

Well, I'll tell you. They said you were ruining me. That I'd
lost all my sparkle and my effervescence. And that it was all
due to you. I've let you eat me up, just sitting here, pouring
myself into you.

CHRIS

Oh, is that what you've been doing?

SALLY

It's all you want. You're like a vampire. If you don't have
someone around you, you sit about in bars waiting to devour
someone.

CHRIS

Your friends said that?

SALLY

My friends are a lot better than the tatty people you run
around with. All your friends seem to be interested in, is just
flopping into bed.

CHRIS

And since when have you had anything against bed?

SALLY

I haven't anything. So long as it leads somewhere.

CHRIS

You mean not just for the fun of it.

SALLY

That's disgusting. That's like animals. But, you know, Chris, I'll tell you something. I've outgrown you.

CHRIS
(*Turns to her*)

You've *what*?

SALLY

I've gone beyond you. I'd better move away from here.

CHRIS

All right. When?

SALLY

The sooner the better, I should think.

CHRIS

That's fine with me.

SALLY

Good.

CHRIS

So, this is the end for us?

SALLY

Yes. If you want it that way. We'll probably bump into each other somewhere, sometime, I expect.

CHRIS

Well, call me sometime, and ask me around for a cocktail.

SALLY
(*Pausing*)
I never know whether you're being serious, or not.

CHRIS

Try it and find out, if your friends will spare you the time.

SALLY
(*Throwing it at him*)
You know, you make me sick. Good-bye, Chris.

CHRIS
(*Alone*)
What a little bitch she is! Well, I've always known that from the start. No, that's not true. I've flattered myself she was fond of me. Nothing would please me better than to see her whipped. Really whipped. Not that I care a curse what she thinks of my article . . . Well, not much. My literary conceit is proof against anything she could say. It's her criticism of myself. The awful, sexual flair women have for taking the stuffing out of men. It's no good telling myself that Sally had the vocabulary and mind of a twelve-year-old schoolgirl. . . . I mismanaged our interview, right from the beginning. I should have been wonderful, convincing, fatherly, mature. I made the one fatal mistake. I let her see I was jealous. Vulgarly jealous. I feel prickly all over with shame. Friends, indeed! Well, I certainly won't see her again, after all this. Never. Never!

(SALLY *returns, very shattered*.)

SALLY

Chris, something awful's happened. Guess who I met in the street, right outside. I met Mother.

CHRIS

Whose mother?

SALLY

Mine.

CHRIS

I thought you said she was in London.

SALLY

She was. But that call of mine upset her. I suppose I did sound a bit drunk. Anyway, she jumped to conclusions, and into an aeroplane. Chris, you're going to have to do something for me. I've been writing her now and then . . . I mean, they do send me money from time to time. I've never had the nerve to tell you, but I sort of gave her to understand—when I first moved in here—that we were engaged.

CHRIS

That who was engaged?

SALLY

You and I. To be married.

CHRIS

Sally, you didn't!

SALLY

Well, I needed someone who sounded like a good, steady influence—and you were the best I could think of. She's in the sitting-room. I told her this place was all untidy, but she'll be in in a minute. Oh, and her name isn't Mrs. Bowles. It's Mrs. Watson-Courtneidge. That's my real name. Only you can't imagine the Germans pronouncing it.

CHRIS

And I'm supposed to stand by and pretend? Oh, no, Sally.

SALLY

Chris, you've got to. You owe it to me.

CHRIS

For what? For letting me eat you up? I'm sorry. And I'm going to my room.

SALLY

(*Getting in his way*)
If you don't, I'll tell her the most awful things about you.

CHRIS

I'm afraid I don't care. Tell her what you like.

SALLY

(*Pleading*)
Chris, you can't do this to me.

CHRIS

After the things you just said to me? That I made you sick.

SALLY

That was just an expression.

CHRIS

No, Sally. We're through. Quite through.

SALLY

Well, we still can be, after she goes home. Only, help me keep her happy. Don't believe everything I said at first about Mother. She isn't easy. Please, darling. Please!
(*Her arms are around his neck. He struggles to disengage himself. Then Mrs. Watson-Courtneidge comes in. She is a middle-aged English lady, in tweeds. She carries a coat.*)

MRS. WATSON-COURTNEIDGE
(*Catching sight of the embrace*)

Excuse me.

SALLY
(*Extricating herself*)

Oh . . .

MRS. WATSON-COURTNEIDGE

I hope this is Mr. Isherwood.

SALLY

Yes. Christopher.

MRS. WATSON-COURTNEIDGE

I'm Mother.

CHRIS

I imagined that.

MRS. WATSON-COURTNEIDGE

Well—don't I deserve a kiss, too?

CHRIS
(*As* SALLY *looks pleadingly at him*)
Oh—yes, of course.
(*A kiss is performed.*)

MRS. WATSON-COURTNEIDGE

You're not a bit like I imagined you.

CHRIS

Oh, really. How did you imagine me?

MRS. WATSON-COURTNEIDGE

Oh, quite different. So this is your room, Sally. Yes, I can see why you said it was untidy.

SALLY

I got up very late this morning. Fräulein Schneider hasn't really had time to do it.

MRS. WATSON-COURTNEIDGE

I don't imagine she does it very well at the best of times. I've just been having a little talk with her. I can't say I like her very much. And why does she sleep in the sitting-room?

CHRIS

So that she can watch the corner.

MRS. WATSON-COURTNEIDGE

And what happens on the corner?

CHRIS

Oh—*that*!

SALLY

Chris!

MRS. WATSON-COURTNEIDGE

I beg your pardon?

CHRIS
(*Vaguely*)

This and that.

MRS. WATSON-COURTNEIDGE

I should think she'd be much better occupied, looking after . . . (*Dusting the table with her fingers*) that and this! (*She picks up the brandy glass*) Sally, you haven't been drinking brandy, I hope.

SALLY

That's Chris's glass.

MRS. WATSON-COURTNEIDGE

On *your* breakfast tray? Where do *you* live, Mr. Isherwood?

CHRIS

Just across the hall.

MRS. WATSON-COURTNEIDGE
(*Dryly*)

How convenient!

SALLY

What do you mean by that, Mother?

MRS. WATSON-COURTNEIDGE

Sally, dear, I'm not asking for details. There are things one doesn't choose to know. But tell me, you two, when are you getting married?

SALLY

I don't know, Mother. We're happy as—we are. Aren't we, Chris?

CHRIS
(*Grimly*)

Just as we are.

MRS. WATSON-COURTNEIDGE

I can well believe it. But sooner or later, these things have to be—well, shall we say, tidied up. There are some questions I would like to ask you, Mr. Isherwood.

CHRIS

Yes?

MRS. WATSON-COURTNEIDGE

I've read your book.

CHRIS

Oh, really?

MRS. WATSON-COURTNEIDGE

After Sally wrote me the title, I got it from the library—with a good deal of trouble. It's an odd book. Was it a success?

CHRIS

No. Not really.

MRS. WATSON-COURTNEIDGE

That doesn't altogether surprise me. I take it you don't live on your writing?

CHRIS

No. Hardly. (*Warningly*) Sally!

MRS. WATSON-COURTNEIDGE

What do you live on?

CHRIS

I teach English.

MRS. WATSON-COURTNEIDGE

And is that sufficient?

CHRIS

I get by.

MRS. WATSON-COURTNEIDGE

Can two get by?

CHRIS

I'm inclined to doubt it. (*As before, but more so*) *Sally!*

MRS. WATSON-COURTNEIDGE

Well that is not my concern. That will be Sally's father's.

CHRIS

(*Getting no response from Sally*)
Well, now if you'll excuse me, Sally . . .

MRS. WATSON-COURTNEIDGE

Are you not lunching with us?

SALLY

Yes, of course he is.

CHRIS

Sally, I can't.

SALLY

Yes, you can. You were lunching with me.

CHRIS

Look, I think there's something we ought to clear up.

SALLY

No!

MRS. WATSON-COURTNEIDGE

What is that?
(*Silence a moment. Then* CHRIS *gives way.*)

CHRIS

I haven't got any decent clothes.

SALLY

You've got your blue suit.

CHRIS

It's almost in rags by daylight.

MRS. WATSON-COURTNEIDGE

My dear Mr. Isherwood, it's not your clothes we want, it's your company. I know all about your background. Anything you wear will be all right, so long as it is clean.

CHRIS

Well, that's part of the point.

SALLY

(*Pushing him out*)
Go and change, Chris. We'll wait here for you.

CHRIS

(*After a look at her*)
I won't be a minute.
(*He goes.*)

MRS. WATSON-COURTNEIDGE

He's an odd young man, Sally.

SALLY

Oh, I don't know, Mother.

MRS. WATSON-COURTNEIDGE

Tell me, that strange telephone call of yours—how much was Mr. Isherwood involved in it?

SALLY

Involved?

MRS. WATSON-COURTNEIDGE

Had you had a few too many cocktails because of some—well—little quarrel with him?

SALLY

Oh, no, Mother. Chris and I never quarrel.

MRS. WATSON-COURTNEIDGE

Well, in any case, I think you two have been together quite enough for the moment. You had better move into the hotel with me.

SALLY
(Protesting)

No, Mother, I . . .

MRS. WATSON-COURTNEIDGE

Sally, don't answer back. You always answer back. I've begun to realize that things are a little more complicated than I had imagined. Hasn't Mr. Isherwood suggested any date for your wedding?

SALLY

No, Mother, I don't think he has.

MRS. WATSON-COURTNEIDGE

I'm not suggesting he will let you down. He's a gentleman. That's one comfort. But . . .

SALLY
(*Urgently*)

Mother, you've got entirely the wrong idea about Chris and me. We aren't . . .

MRS. WATSON-COURTNEIDGE
(*Interrupting her*)

Sally, that is something you might have had to say to your grandmother. You don't have to say it to me.

SALLY

But, Mother . . .

MRS. WATSON-COURTNEIDGE
(*As before*)

Mother's quite broad-minded.

SALLY
(Giving way)

Well, all right, but don't rush him. Don't try and force him, or anything.

MRS. WATSON-COURTNEIDGE

Trust Mother! I see you still have that picture. You had that in the nursery. "The Kitten's Awakening." I'm glad you still have that. The old things are still the best, after all, aren't they?

SALLY
(Subdued)

Yes, Mother.

MRS. WATSON-COURTNEIDGE
(Embracing her)

We must get you back to them.

Curtain

ACT THREE

Scene II

Scene: *The same. Afternoon. About three days later.*
At rise: FRITZ *is on stage.* FRÄULEIN SCHNEIDER *is setting a tray of coffee for him. The old pictures are back on the walls. The room is again as in Scene I.*

FRÄULEIN SCHNEIDER

He is always back around this time, Herr Wendel. You cannot have to wait long.

FRITZ

I am glad that Christopher could move back into this room again. Will he stay on here?

FRÄULEIN SCHNEIDER

Oh, I hope. He is doing better now. Starting new lessons. It is true they are almost all to the Jews, but even so there is at least some good that comes from them that way. (FRITZ *does not answer*) Is it true, Herr Wendel, that they will take the money away from the Jews, and drive them all out?

FRITZ

I have no idea.

154

FRÄULEIN SCHNEIDER

It would be a good thing. Do you not agree with me?

FRITZ

I don't really know.

FRÄULEIN SCHNEIDER

But you must know, Herr Wendel. That is what the speakers all say. Everyone must know, and everyone must agree and only then can Germany be saved.

(*Voices heard offstage.*)

CHRIS'S VOICE

Go right in there, Natalia. Are you sure you're all right?

NATALIA'S VOICE

Oh, yes, I thank you. I am all right.

CHRIS'S VOICE

And then come to my room. It's the old room.

(*He comes in. He is a little more messed up than usual*)

Oh, hello, Fritz. I didn't know you were here.

(FRÄULEIN SCHNEIDER *goes out.*)

FRITZ

Was that Natalia's voice I heard outside?

CHRIS

Yes, she's gone to the bathroom. I must wash my hands.

FRITZ

What is the matter?

CHRIS

There was a bit of trouble.
(*He pours water into the basin.*)

FRITZ

But what is it all about?

CHRIS
(*Washing his hands*)
I was walking with Natalia after her lesson. We ran into a
bunch of toughs. Nazis, of course. They were holding a street
meeting. And Natalia insisted on joining in.

FRITZ

Joining in?

CHRIS

Yes, she got quite fierce. She made a speech. She was almost
like Joan of Arc. I was quite astonished.

FRITZ

She is wonderful, that girl.

CHRIS

And she was hit in the face with a stone.

FRITZ

Um Gotteswillen.

CHRIS

It wasn't serious. At least, I don't think it was. I wanted her to go to a doctor, but she wouldn't. I think she is a bit shaken, that's all. And this place was nearer than her home. I brought her here.

FRITZ

It is better perhaps if your landlady does not see her.

CHRIS

Why?

FRITZ

She is not very partial to the Jews, your landlady.

CHRIS

Yes, I know. But she doesn't know what she is talking about.

FRITZ

She knows as much as most people.

CHRIS

And that is the tragedy.
(CHRIS *takes a series of Band-Aids, and starts to put them on his hands rather excessively.*)

FRITZ

What is with your hands? Were you in it too?

CHRIS

Well, after Natalia started, I couldn't really keep out of it. Trying to get her away.

FRITZ

Natalia should not stay here.

CHRIS

She'll stay as long as her father stays.

FRITZ

She would go if she married.

CHRIS

I doubt that.

FRITZ

(*Urgently*)

But she ought to go! Christopher, I know now I am in love with Natalia. I have not seen her, but I am in love with her.

(NATALIA *enters. There is a small scar, newly washed, on her face.*)

NATALIA

So, Christopher, I think now . . .

(*She sees* FRITZ, *and stops*)

Oh, Fritz.

FRITZ

Ja, Natalia.

NATALIA

Christopher did not tell me you were here.

FRITZ

He did not know.

CHRIS

Let me give you some brandy, Natalia.

NATALIA

I do not think so.

CHRIS

Yes, but I do think so. You need something. And it's quite good brandy. It's part of—quite a good loot. I'm going to have some.

FRITZ
(*To* NATALIA)

Please, may I see your face?

NATALIA
(*Turning*)

There is nothing there.

FRITZ

(*Kneeling*)

I would like to see, please. It is clean? You have washed it?
You have washed it thoroughly?

NATALIA

I have washed it thoroughly.

CHRIS

Would you like to put a Band-Aid on it?

NATALIA

On my face?

CHRIS

I think you should. You can get blood poisoning.

NATALIA

And a bandage will help that?

CHRIS

I have some iodine. I can put that on for you.

NATALIA

Not on my face, I thank you.

FRITZ

You let me put one of these on. Just a very small one.
Like so.

(*He holds one up.*)

NATALIA
(Touched, but unwilling to show it)
I can put it on myself.

FRITZ
I know, but let me do it, please. You drink your brandy, and let me do it.
(He starts to do so.)

CHRIS
(Looking at his hands)
You know, I wonder if I shouldn't take these Band-Aids off, and put on some iodine. I could get gangrene.

NATALIA
No, Christopher, you could not.

CHRIS
You never know. Then they amputate your hands. And you can't write or type any more.
(He tears off the Band-Aids and paints on iodine.)

FRITZ
(Finishing his job)
There.
(He seems to feel a little faint)
Now *I* take some brandy.
(He and NATALIA gulp some, hastily.)

NATALIA
And now I think I go home.

FRITZ

You let me take you, please.

NATALIA

My dear young man, I . . .

FRITZ

(*Finishing for her*)

I am not yet sixty years old, and I can go home unmolested.

NATALIA

I prefer that I go alone.

FRITZ

I would like that you let me take you.

NATALIA

And if we run into another of these street riots?

FRITZ

I would still like to take you.
    (CHRIS *raises his head. The two men exchange glances.*
    FRITZ *nods very gently*)
I tell it now.

CHRIS

Let him take you, Natalia. I would feel better.

NATALIA

Very well. I see you tomorrow, Christopher. At the usual
hour.

CHRIS

Yes, of course. Good-bye, Natalia. I admired you very much
this afternoon.

FRITZ

I, too.

NATALIA

I cannot see why. Come.
(*She goes out with* FRITZ.)
(CHRIS *looks after them, then picks up the Band-Aids
and the iodine, and resumes his painting.*)

CHRIS

It doesn't look too good.
(*He splashes on some more iodine.*)
(FRÄULEIN SCHNEIDER *comes in.*)

FRÄULEIN SCHNEIDER

I take the coffee tray. What is with your hands, Herr Issyvoo?

CHRIS

I think they may be poisoned.

FRÄULEIN SCHNEIDER

But how did you come to hurt them?

CHRIS

It was in a street riot.

FRÄULEIN SCHNEIDER

An anti-Jewish riot?

CHRIS

Yes.

FRÄULEIN SCHNEIDER

And you were attacking the Jews.

CHRIS

No, I was doing the other thing. I was defending them.

FRÄULEIN SCHNEIDER

But that is not right, Herr Issyvoo. The Jews are at the bottom of all the trouble.

CHRIS
(Sharply)

Fräulein Schneider, I think I've heard enough of that this afternoon. Let's not talk about it any more.

FRÄULEIN SCHNEIDER

But that is wrong, Herr Issyvoo. We must all talk about it. That is what the speakers say. Germany must come first.

CHRIS
(*Turning angrily*)

And what does that mean? How can any country come
first that does things like that? Suppose I push this in your
face
(*He thrusts his fist near her face, and she retreats*)
because Germany must come first—and I'm strong enough to
do it, and to hurt you? What does that prove?

FRÄULEIN SCHNEIDER

But, Herr Issyvoo . . .

CHRIS

I've always been fond of you. Now I'm ashamed of you.
And everything you say is horrible and dangerous and abom-
inable. And now please go away.

FRÄULEIN SCHNEIDER
(*Angrily*)

You will see, Herr Issyvoo. You will see.
(*Bell rings.*)

CHRIS

I know that talking like this makes me almost as bad as
you. Or perhaps worse. Because I've got intelligence—I hope—
and you've just been listening to things. Now go and answer
the bell. (*She goes. He cries out in exasperation to himself*)
God, what is one supposed to do? (*He examines his hands
again*) I wonder if I've broken anything. It feels awfully loose.
(*He flexes his thumb*) Ought that to move like that, or
oughtn't it?

(SALLY *comes in. She wears the coat her mother was
carrying in the previous scene.*)

SALLY

Hello, Chris.

CHRIS

Well, fancy seeing you again, without your mother.
(MRS. WATSON-COURTNEIDGE *comes in.*)

CHRIS

Oh, hello, Mrs. Watson-Courtneidge!

MRS. WATSON-COURTNEIDGE

Good afternoon, Christopher.

CHRIS

And how are things with you two?

MRS. WATSON-COURTNEIDGE

They're very well. Sally has been making me very happy.

CHRIS

I see you've dressed her up in your clothes.

SALLY
(*Defensively*)

What's wrong with that? Mother's got very good taste.

CHRIS

But it's hardly *your* taste, is it?

MRS. WATSON-COURTNEIDGE
(*Lifting the glass*)

Brandy again?

CHRIS
(*Defiantly*)

Yes.

MRS. WATSON-COURTNEIDGE

I see. What's the matter with your hands?

CHRIS

I hurt them. I was in a fight.

SALLY

Good gracious, you! What was the fight about?

CHRIS

Jews.

MRS. WATSON-COURTNEIDGE

Why were you fighting about *them*?

CHRIS

I don't like seeing people being pushed around.
(*To* SALLY)
Or made to pretend they're what they're not.

MRS. WATSON-COURTNEIDGE

Oh, I see. Well, now, Christopher, there's something I want
to tell you. I'm taking Sally home.

CHRIS

Oh? And what do *you* say about that, Sally?

SALLY

Mother's quite right, Chris. She really is. I ought to go home. To my past, and my roots and things. They're very important to a girl.

CHRIS

Sally, don't. Don't let her!

SALLY

Let her what?

CHRIS

You're disappearing, right in front of my eyes.

MRS. WATSON-COURTNEIDGE

I hope the girl you knew *is* disappearing. I want you to come, too, Christopher. Then you can meet Sally's father, and, if he approves of you, he will find you a job of some sort. Then you can be married from our house at the end of next month. That will give me time to arrange Sally's trousseau.

CHRIS

Look, Sally, haven't you told your mother yet?

SALLY
(*Miserably*)

No, not yet.

MRS. WATSON-COURTNEIDGE

Told me what?

CHRIS

Sally, I think you should.

SALLY
(*Desperately*)

No, Chris, not now.

CHRIS

Yes, now. Mrs. Courtneidge, there's something I have to tell you. Sally and I are no longer engaged. She sent me a note this morning, to break it off.

MRS. WATSON-COURTNEIDGE

Sally, you never told me.

SALLY
(*Very relieved*)

I wanted to speak to Chris first.

MRS. WATSON-COURTNEIDGE

This is all a little sudden.

CHRIS

I don't think it's very sudden, really. We had a sort of quarrel the morning you arrived, and we never really made it up since.

MRS. WATSON-COURTNEIDGE

I thought you never quarreled.

CHRIS

Who said that?

MRS. WATSON-COURTNEIDGE

Sally did. Are you sure about this, Sally?

SALLY

Well, yes, Mother, as a matter of fact, I am. I don't think Chris and I are really suited to each other.

MRS. WATSON-COURTNEIDGE

Neither do I. But I didn't expect you to realize it. Well, this alters everything. I will not expect *you* to come back to England, Christopher.

CHRIS

Good.

MRS. WATSON-COURTNEIDGE

But I'm very glad that Sally has been able to see the truth for herself. I was afraid that she had changed almost too much. That *you* had changed her.

SALLY
(*To* CHRIS)

See?

MRS. WATSON-COURTNEIDGE
(*To* SALLY)

Now you'll come back and settle down again, and quite soon all of this will be forgotten. I'm sure it will seem like a rather bitter experience, but one gets over everything in the right surroundings.

SALLY
(*Subdued again*)

Yes, Mother.

MRS. WATSON-COURTNEIDGE

She has been very good about you, Christopher. She has continued to deny everything that I am absolutely sure has taken place. I think that shows a very fine character.

CHRIS

No doubt that was due to *your* influence.

MRS. WATSON-COURTNEIDGE

Perhaps you'll forgive me if I say a few things to you, Christopher. I think someone should say them, and Sally's father isn't here to do so. Perhaps that's lucky for you. He's not a patient man, and he adores Sally. I know he'd think that anyone who'd harmed her richly deserved a sound horse-whipping.

CHRIS

Now, listen, Mrs. Courtneidge . . .

MRS. WATSON-COURTNEIDGE

I have no intention of listening to you, Mr. Isherwood. Sally has done quite enough of that, already. She's a very sweet, simple girl, but she's too easily influenced.

CHRIS
(*With meaning*)

Yes, I know.

MRS. WATSON-COURTNEIDGE

Perhaps you think I'm a simple woman, too. Perhaps you think I haven't noticed that, while you've dragged me to the opera and all the museums, you have never introduced me to a single one of your friends. I can well imagine why.

CHRIS

Look, do we have to go into all this?

MRS. WATSON-COURTNEIDGE
(*Sharply*)

Yes, I think we do. It's people like you who are ruining the world. Unprincipled drifters who call themselves authors, never write a word, and then vote Labor on the slightest provocation. No wonder we're headed for socialism. You live in foreign countries, and you let yourself get involved in obscure political issues that are no concern of yours . . .

SALLY
(*Suddenly*)

Yes, they are.

MRS. WATSON-COURTNEIDGE
(*Surprised*)

Sally!

SALLY

Some sort of principles are, and I'm very glad to see he has some, and that there is something he is willing to fight for, instead of just sitting around.

CHRIS

Now, Sally, wait a minute. . . .

SALLY

I know. I've told you a lot of the same things, myself. But I don't like to hear Mother say them. Certainly not to you. You don't know Chris, Mother. You don't understand him. He's a very fine person. He's been wonderful to me. He has. He's done a lot for me, and he's tried to do more. And he's an artist. Well—potentially. All artists need time. He's going to write a wonderful book one day, that'll sell millions of copies—or a lot of short stories all about Germany or something—which will tell the world wonderful things about life and people and everything—and then you'll feel very silly for the things you've just said.

MRS. WATSON-COURTNEIDGE

I thought you'd just broken off your engagement.

SALLY

Yes, I have. But I'm not going to stand here and let you nag at him like that. He doesn't chase around after horrible, influential people, and I bet he wouldn't take a job from

Father if he offered him one. He's got too much pride. And character. It just wants—working up, that's all. And now let's go.

MRS. WATSON-COURTNEIDGE
(*Staggered*)
Well . . . I'll say good-bye, Christopher. We shall be leaving tomorrow, or the next day. I don't imagine that we'll meet again. And I would prefer that you and Sally did not see each other again, either. Shall we go, Sally?

SALLY
Yes, Mother.
      (*They leave,* SALLY *refusing to look back at* CHRIS.)

CHRIS
Well. Really! (*He goes to the table, and the brandy bottle, then stops*) No, I won't. I *will* have some principles!

Curtain

ACT THREE

Scene III

TIME: *Three days later. Evening.*
SCENE: *A large trunk is open in the middle of the floor.*
CHRIS *is putting things into it and sorting others from the*
closet.

CHRIS

Where did I ever get all these things? This shirt—I can't
possibly have bought it. No, I didn't, of course. I remember.
It was at that party at the Lithuanian sculptor's, where a whole
bottle of crème de menthe got spilled over mine. These are
Clive's silk ones. I don't suppose I'll ever wear them, but you
never know. This pair of drawers. No, really, they're too far
gone. Out!

> (*He throws them away. Enter* SALLY. *She is dressed as*
> *in the first scene.*)

SALLY

Chris!

CHRIS

Sally! I thought you'd gone. I thought you'd gone home.

SALLY

No. Mother left this morning.

CHRIS

And you're not going?

SALLY

Not home. Oh, Chris, it was ghastly getting rid of Mother. But I knew I had to, after that scene here.

CHRIS

How did you do it?

SALLY
(*Giggling*)
I did something awful. I got a friend in London to send her an anonymous telegram telling her Daddy was having an affair. That sent her off in a mad whirl. But Daddy will forgive me. Besides, it's probably true—and I don't blame him. I told Mother I'd follow her when I got some business settled. And something will turn up to stop it. It always does, for me I'm all right, Chris. I'm back again.

CHRIS
(*Smiling*)
Yes. I can see you are.

SALLY

Is there anything to drink?

CHRIS

There's just a little gin, that's all.

SALLY

I'd love a little gin. In a tooth glass. Flavored with peppermint. Where are you off to?

CHRIS

I *am* going home.

SALLY

When?

CHRIS

Tomorrow night. I'm going to Fritz and Natalia's wedding in the afternoon.

SALLY

Wedding? How did that happen?

CHRIS

Fritz told Natalia about himself, and that did it. And now he doesn't have to pretend any more. Come with me, Sally. They'd love to see you.

SALLY

Oh, I'd like to, but I won't be here.

CHRIS

Where will you be?

SALLY

I'm leaving for the Riviera tonight.

CHRIS

With whom?

SALLY

For a picture.

CHRIS

Well, fine. Is it a good part?

SALLY

I don't really know. I expect so. You haven't got a drink, Chris. Have a drop of this. Make it a loving cup.
(*He takes a sip*)
Why are you going away, Chris?

CHRIS

Because I'll never write as long as I'm here. And I've got to write. It's the only thing I give a damn about. I don't regret the time I've spent here. I wouldn't have missed a single hangover of it. But now I've got to put it all down—what I think about it. And live by it, too, if I can. Thank you for the idea about that book, Sally. The short stories. I think maybe that will work out.

SALLY

Oh, I hope so. I do want you to be good, Chris.

CHRIS

I am going to try, Sally. Now, tell me about you and this job that you don't seem to know anything about. Or care about. Who's the man, Sally?

SALLY

Man?

CHRIS

Oh, come off it.

SALLY
(*Giggling a little*)
Well, there is a man. He's wonderful, Chris. He really is.

CHRIS

Where did you meet him?

SALLY

Two days ago. Just after we left here. He saw us in the street. . . . Mother and me, I mean—and our eyes met—his and mine, I mean—and he sort of followed us. To a tea shop, where he sat and gazed at me. And back to the hotel. And at the restaurant. He had the table next to us, and he kept sort of hitching his foot around my chair. And he passed me a note in the fruit-basket. Only Mother got it by mistake. But it was in German. I told her it was from a movie agent. And I went over and talked to him, and he *was*! Then we met later. He's quite marvelous, Chris. He's got a long, black beard. Well, not really long. I've never been kissed by a beard before. I thought it would be awful. But it isn't. It's quite exciting. Only he doesn't speak much German. He's a Yugoslavian. That's why I don't know much about the picture. But I'm sure it will be all right. He'll write in something. And now I've got to run.

CHRIS

Oh, Sally, *must* you? Must you go on like this? Why don't you go home, too? Come back with me. I mean it, Sally. My family'll give me some money if I'm home. Or I'll get a job. I'll see that you're all right.

SALLY

It wouldn't be any good, Chris. I'd run away from you, too. The moment anything attractive came along. It's all right for you. You're a writer. You really are. I'm not even an actress, really. I'd love to see my name in lights, but even if I had a first-night tomorrow, if something exciting turned up, I'd go after it. I can't help it. That's me. I'm sentimental enough to hope that one day I'll meet the perfect man, and marry him and have an enormous family and be happy, but until then— well, that's how I am. You know that really, don't you?

CHRIS

Yes, Sally, I'm afraid I do.

SALLY

Afraid? Oh, Chris, am I too awful—for *me,* I mean?

CHRIS

No, Sally. I'm very fond of you.

SALLY

I do hope you are. Because I am of you. Was it true about eternal friendship that we swore?

CHRIS

Yes, of course it was. Really true. Tell me, do you have an address?

SALLY

No, I don't. But I'll write. I really will. Postcards and everything. And you write to me. Of course, you'll be writing all sorts of things—books and things—that I can read. Will you dedicate one to me?

CHRIS

The very first one.

SALLY

Oh, good. Perhaps that'll be my only claim to fame. Well—good-bye for now, Chris. Neck and leg-break.

CHRIS

Neck and leg-break.
    (*They go into each other's arms.*)

SALLY
        (*Starts to go, then turns to* CHRIS)
I do love you.
    (*She goes, swiftly.*)

CHRIS
(*Stares after her, for a moment*)

I love you too, Sally. And it's so damned stupid that that's not enough to keep two people together.

(*He starts to move toward the window. The lights begin to dim*)

The camera's taken all its pictures, and now it's going away to develop them. I wonder how Sally will look when I've developed her? I haven't got an end for her yet, but there probably isn't one. She'll just go on and on, as she always has—somewhere.

(*He looks out of the window*)

There she goes now. Into the photograph. She's just going around the corner.

(*He watches as the curtain starts to fall*)

Don't forget those postcards, Sally.

Curtain